The Poems of Alexander Scott.

Early English Text Society.
Extra Series, LXXXV.
1902.

The Poems

of

Alexander Scott.

EDITED FROM THE BANNATYNE MANUSCRIPT IN THE
ADVOCATES' LIBRARY, EDINBURGH, AND THE MAITLAND
MANUSCRIPT IN THE LIBRARY OF MAGDALEN
COLLEGE, CAMBRIDGE,

BY

ALEXANDER KARLEY DONALD.

LONDON:
PUBLISHED FOR THE EARLY ENGLISH TEXT SOCIETY
BY KEGAN PAUL, TRENCH, TRÜBNER & CO., LIMITED,
PATERNOSTER HOUSE, CHARING CROSS ROAD, W.C.
1902.

OXFORD
UNIVERSITY PRESS

Great Clarendon Street, Oxford OX2 6DP
United Kingdom

Oxford University Press is a department of the University of Oxford.
It furthers the University's objective of excellence in research, scholarship,
and education by publishing worldwide. Oxford is a registered trade mark of
Oxford University Press in the UK and in certain other countries

© The Early English Text Society 1902

The moral rights of the authors have been asserted

Database right Oxford University Press (maker)

First Edition published in 1902

All rights reserved. No part of this publication may be reproduced,
stored in a retrieval system, or transmitted, in any form or by any means,
without the prior permission in writing of Oxford University Press,
or as expressly permitted by law, or under terms agreed with the appropriate
reprographics rights organization. Enquiries concerning reproduction
outside the scope of the above should be sent to the Rights Department,
Oxford University Press, at the address above

You must not circulate this book in any other form
and you must impose this same condition on any acquirer

Published in the United States of America by Oxford University Press
198 Madison Avenue, New York, NY 10016, United States of America

British Library Cataloguing in Publication Data
Data available

Library of Congress Cataloging in Publication Data
Data available

Extra Series, 85

ISBN 978-0-85-991995-1

TABLE OF CONTENTS.

	PAGE
Introduction	vii
Index of First Lines	xi
George Bannatyne's Epistle to the Reader	1
1. Ane New Yeir Gift to the Quene Mary	3
2. The justing and debait vp at the Drum, betuix Wm Adamsone, and Johnie Sym	10
3. Of May	16
4. O lusty May, with Flora Quene	18

Poems on the Pains and Pleasures of Love.

5. Luve preysis, but comparesone	19
6. Haif hairt in hairt, ye hairt of hairtis, haill (Anon.) ...	20
7. The anschir to the ballat of hairtis	21
8. Hence, hairt, with hir that mvst departe	22
9. Quha is perfyte to put in wryt	23
10. I wil be plane and lufe affane	25
11. Only to yow in erd that I lufe best	26
12. Rycht as the glass bene thirlit thrucht with bemis ...	27
13. Vp, helsum hairt! thy rutis rais, and lowp	28
14. How suld my febill body fure?	29
15. Marvilling in mynd, quhat ailis fortoun at me? ...	30
16. Departe, departe, departe	32
17. That evir I luvit, allace thairfoir	34
18. Oppressit hairt, indure	35
19. Leif luve, and lat me leif allone	37
20. Thocht I in grit distress	38
21. Langour to leive, allace	40

		PAGE
22.	Favour is fair in luvis lair	41
23.	Returne thee, hairt, hamewart agane	42
24.	In June the jem of joy and geme	43
25.	Thair is nocht ane winche that I se	44
26.	Quod Scott quhen his wyfe left him	45
27.	Quha lykis to luve or that law pruve	46
28.	Lo! quhat it is to luve	47
29.	Quhome sould I wyt of my mischance	48
30.	It cumis yow luvaris to be laill	49
31.	Fra raige of yowth the rynk hes rune	51

Satires.

32.	The slicht remeid of luve	53
33.	Ane ballat maid to the derisioun and scorne of wantoun wemen	55
34.	I mvse and mervillis in my mind	58
35.	Ladies, be war that plesand ar	60
36.	Ye blindit luvaris, luke	61

Paraphrases of the Psalms.

37.	The first Psalme	66
38.	The fyifty Psalme	67
	The Wryttar to the Redare by George Bannatyne	70

	Notes and Illustrations	71
	Glossary	95
	Index of Proper Names	111

INTRODUCTION.

THE monks at a certain monastery were accustomed to listen at meal-times to a discourse on the life of one of the deceased members of their order. One day the reader gave out a name unfamiliar to them all, and he alarmed the hungry brethren by announcing that he would group his remarks under three headings. Firstly, What do we know of our deceased brother? Secondly, is his history authentic? Thirdly, can further light be expected? The alarm that dinner would grow cold was dispelled, as the reader proceeded to say that under the first head he had but one observation—That we know very little about the deceased brother; and as to the second, he stated that the little we did know was very doubtful; and under the third, his only remark was that it was extremely unlikely we shall ever know more. It is an unpleasant fact that this discourse might be made concerning several Scottish writers, and on none more appropriately than Alexander Scott.

His Poems are preserved mainly in the manuscript collection of Scottish poetry, which was made in 1568 by George Bannatyne to while away a time of enforced retirement when the city of Edinburgh was suffering from a visitation of plague. This enables us to say that the poems were all written before 1568. So far as I know Alexander Scott's name is not referred to in the writings of his contemporaries.[1] It is hardly possible to fix the dates of any of the

---

[1] David Irving, *The History of Scottish Poetry*, p. 418, quotes the lines below as perhaps referring to Scott. It is doubtful if they do. We do not know the date of the sonnet, though it cannot have been written much before 1570, as Montgomery was born about 1545.

    Ye knaw ill guyding genders mony gees, [aberrations]
    And specially in poets: for example,
    Ye can pen out tua cuple and ye pleis,
  Yourself and I, old Scot and Robert Semple :
    Quhen we ar dead, that all our dayis bot daffis,
    Let Christian Lyndesay wryt our epitaphis.

poems by internal evidence, except *The New Yeir Gift*. In the poem, *Quha lykis to luve*, there is a reference to an epidemic of plague then said to be raging: this may refer the poem to 1529, which was the first year in the century in which plague was rampant in Edinburgh, and it did not break out again until the time Bannatyne made his transcript of Scottish verse in 1568. The *Lament of the Maister of Erskyn* may refer to the Master of Erskyn who lost his life at the battle of Pinkie in 1547. From what Knox[1] says of him it seems that he was a man well known in society, and the *Lament* may have been written after the news of his fate had reached the capital. The poem of May has a reference to the dramatic entertainment of Robin Hood. There was a notable disturbance of the peace in Edinburgh in 1560 over this forbidden pastime, and it may be that the fifth stanza of the poem is an allusion to that event. Then there comes the verses to Queen Mary on her return to Scotland, and we may safely refer them to 1561, and judging from the matter of the verses we are inclined to think that they are the production of a man who had reached years of maturity and discernment, and who had become reminiscent.

I think it may be conjectured that Scott was born some time in the reign of James IV., and that he lived down to the time of Queen Mary, or perhaps to early in the reign of James VI.

Scott's love poems are among the best produced in Scotland in the sixteenth century. Some of them express in melodious verse genuine feeling; and there is a vein of sly humour which warns the fair ones not to give too much trouble in wooing. It was this gaiety of disposition which made Pinkerton speak of Scott as the Scottish Anacreon.

The satirical poems indicate a very low state of morals among both sexes; but Scott is not the only Scottish poet who castigates his countrymen. The reforming divines used to ascribe the low state of morals to French influences introduced by Queen Mary, at least such was the opinion Knox expressed in his *History of the Reformation*, Book IV., in a passage of sufficient interest to deserve quotation.

"In the verie tyme of the Generall Assemblie, thair cumis to publyct knawlege ane heinous murdour committed in the Courte, yea, not far from the Quenis awin lap; for ane Frenche woman, that servit in the Queneis chalmer had playit the hure with the Quenis

---

[1] *History of the Reformation*, Guthrie's Ed., 1898, at p. 87.

awin hipoticary. The woman conceveit and bare ane child quhome with commoune consent the father and the mother murthered. Yit wer the cryis of ane new borne barne hard; searche wes maid, the chylde and mowther wes baith deprehendit, and so wer baith the man and the woman dampned to be hangit upoun the publict streit of Edinburgh. The punischment was notable, because the cryme wes heinous. Bot yit wes not the courte purged of hureis and huredome, quhilk wes the fontane of sik enormiteis, for it wes weill knawin that schame haistit the mariage betwixt Johne sempill, callit the Danser, and Marie Levingstoune, surnameit the Lustie. What bruit the Maries and the rest of the dansaris of the Courte had the ballatis of that aige did witnes, quhilk we for modesteis sake omit. Bot this wes the commoune complaint of all godlie and wyse men, that giff thai thochht that sick ane Courte soulde lang continew, and giff thai luikit for no uther lyffe to cum, thay wald haif wissit thair soneis and dochteris rather to have bene brought up with fydlars and dansaris, and to have bene exerceit in flinging upone ane flure, and in the rest that thairof followis, than to haif bene nurisched in the companie of the godlie & exerceissit in vertew, quhilk in that Courte wes haittit, and fylthines not onlie maintenit, bot also rewairded. Witnes the Lordschip of Abercorne, the baronie of Authormortie, & diverse utheris pertenyng to the patrimonie of the Crowne, gyffin heritage to scouparis [skippers] dansaris, and dalliaris with damis. This wes the begyning of the regement of Marie Quene of Scottis, and thir wer the fructeis that sche brocht furth of France."

Whether Queen Mary really was responsible for a deterioration of morals is doubtful, as we find Dunbar in the reign of James IV. writing in a similar strain to Scott before Mary was born. The poem, *To luve vnluvit it is ane pane,* seems to show that Scott's wife was unfaithful; perhaps this embittered his feelings and caused him to denounce womankind in general. The satirical poems are not pessimistic; the poet seems to revel in unmasking the vices of the time; whether his victims amend or not, he is determined to publish their failings on the housetops.

Ane New Yeir Gift shows Scott to have been on the side of the reformation. The literature of the earlier generation was full of the wrongs suffered by the labouring classes. The *Complainte of Scotlande* sets forth how they were harassed by the clergy and the nobility; but the reformation movement did not mend matters, and Scott bitterly denounces the rapacity of those who under the pretence of religious reforms had seized the church lands, and placed a heavier burden on the backs of the peasants than they had to bear before.

Scott's poems have been several times printed. Allan Ramsay inserted seven in the *Evergreen,* 1724; Lord Hailes printed seven in

Ancient Scottish Poems, 1770; and James Sibbald in a *Chronicle of Scottish Poetry*, 1802, printed fifteen. There are three editions which are nearly complete. One by David Laing published in 1821; an edition printed for private circulation in Glasgow in 1882; and one by the Scottish Text Society, edited by Dr. James Cranstoun, which is by far the best of the three. There is also a modernized version of a number of the poems by William Mackean, Paisley, 1887.

I am bound to record my thanks to my friends, Alexander Morton, M.A., Kirkaldy, for the very valuable aid rendered in the preparation of this edition, especially in connection with the glossary, and James Pittendrigh MacGillivray, R.S.A., Edinburgh, for the drawings which decorate the volume.

Bombay, Christmas 1900.

INDEX OF FIRST LINES.

	PAGE
Considdir, hairt, my trew intent	21
Departe, departe, departe	32
Favour is fair in luvis lair	41
Fra raige of yowth the rynk hes rune	51
Haif hairt in hairt, ye hairt of hairtis, haill	20
Happie is hie hes hald him fre	66
Hence, hairt, with hir that most departe	22
How suld my febill body fure?	29
I mvse and mervellis in my mind	58
I wil be plane and lufe affane	25
In June the jem of joy and geme	43
It cumis yow luvaris to be laill	49
Ladeis, be war that plesand ar	60
Langour to leive, allace	40
Leif luve and lat me leif allone	37
Lo, quhat it is to lufe	47
Lord God deliuer me, allace!	67
Luvaris, lat be the frennessy of luve	53
Luve preysis, but comparesone	19
Marvilling in mynd, quhat ailis fortoun at me	30
May is the moneth maist amene	16
O lusty May, with Flora quene	18
Only to yow in erd that I lufe best	26
Oppressit hairt, indure	35
Quha is perfyte to put in wryt	23

Index of First Lines.

	PAGE
Quha lykis to luve, or that law pruve	46
Quhome sould I wyt of my mischance	48
Returne the, hairt, hamewart agane	42
Rycht as the glass bene thirlit thrucht with bemis	27
Thair is nocht ane winche þat I se	44
That evir I luvit, allace thairfoir	34
The grit debait and turnament	10
Thocht I in grit distress	38
To luve vnluvit it is ane pane	45
Vp, helsum hairt! thy rutis rais, and lowp	28
Welcum, illustrat ladye, and oure quene!	3
Ye blindit luvaris, luke	61
Ye lusty ladyis luke	55

The Wryttar to the Reidaris.

Ye reverend redaris, thir workis revolving richt,
Gif ye get crymis, correct thame to your micht
And curse na clark that cunnyngly thame wrait,
Bot blame me, baldly brocht this buik till licht
In tenderest tyme, quhen knawlege was nocht bricht,
Bot lait begun to lerne and till translait
My copeis awld, mankit, and mvtillait;
Quhais trewth, as standis, yit haif I, sympill wicht,
Tryd furth, thairfoir excuse sumpairt my estait.

                                          [George Bannatyne.]

1.

Ane new ȝeir gift, to the quene Mary, Quhen scho come first hame.

[19th August, 1561.]

Welcum! illustrat ladye, and oure quene;	1 [If. 90, p. 241] Welcome illustrious lady and our queen.
Welcum! oure lyone with þe floure de lyce;	
Welcum! oure thrissill with þe lorane grene;	
Welcum! oure rubent roiss vpoun þe ryce;	
Welcum! oure jem and joyfull genetryce; 5	
Welcum! oure beill of albion to beir;	
Welcum! oure plesand princes, maist of pryce;	
God gif þe grace aganis þis guid new-ȝeir. 8	
This guid new ȝeir, we hoip, with grace of god, 9	We hope this year will be peaceful,
Sal be of peax, tranquillitie, and rest;	
This ȝeir sall rycht and ressone rewle þe rod,	and that right and reason, too long suppressed, will reign.
Quhilk sa lang seasoun hes bene soir supprest;	
This ȝeir, ferme fayth sall frelie be confest, 13	
And all erronius questionis put areir,	
To lauboure þat þis lyfe amang ws lest;	
God gif þe grace aganis þis guid new-ȝeir. 16	
Heirfore addres the dewlie to decoir, 17	
And rewle thy regne with hie magnificence.	
Begin at God to gar sett furth his gloir,	Beg God to set forth His glory, and get experience of His gospel, and cause His true Church to be reverenced.
And of his gospell gett experience,	
Caus his trew kirk be had in reuerence; 21	
So sall thy name and fame spred far and neir:	
Now, this thy dett to do with diligence,	
God gif þe grace aganis þis guid new-ȝeir. 24	

4   *Ane New Yeir Gift to the Quene Mary.*   [1.

<small>Found thy reign on Wisdom, Justice, Fortitude, and Temperance.</small>

Found on þe first four vertewus cardinall,   25
On wisdome, iustice, force, and temperans;
Applaud to prudent men, and principall
Off virtewus lyfe, thy wirschep till avance;
Waye iustice equale, without discrepance;   29
Strenth thy estait with steidfastnes to steir;
To temper tyme with trew continuance,
God gife þe grace aganis þis guid new-ȝeir.   32

<small>Take counsel of the wise. Cleave to Christ.</small>

Cast thy consate be counsale of þe sage,   33
And cleif to christ, hes kepit þe in cure,
Attingent now to twentye ȝeir of aige,
Preservand þe fra all misaventure.

<small>Watch affairs with your own eyes. Protect the poor.</small>

Wald thow be servit, and thy cuntre sure?   37
Still on þe commounweill haif E and eir;
Preiss ay to be protectrix of þe pure;
So god sall gyde thy grace this gude new-ȝeir.   40

<small>Staunch strife in thy estates, stablish them in constancy and love. [leaf 90 b, p. 242] Banish quarrels between the clergy and laymen. Make thy prelates live honest lives.</small>

Gar stanche all stryiff, and stabill thy estaitis   41
In constance, concord, cherite, and lufe;
Be bissie now to banisch all debatis,
Betuix kirkmen and temporall men dois mufe;
The pulling doun of policie reprufe,   45
And lat perversit prelettis leif perqueir;
To do the best, besekand god above,
To gife the grace aganis þis guid new-ȝeir.   48

<small>Proclaim that none but the learned shall be allowed to dispute about Holy Writ.</small>

Att croce gar cry be oppin proclamatioun,   49
Vndir grit panis, þat nothir he nor scho,
Off halye writ, haif ony disputatioun
Bot letterit men, or lernit clerkis þerto;
For lymmer lawdis, and litle lassis lo,   53
Will argūn bayth with bischop, preist, and freir:
To dantoun þis, thow hes aneuch to do,
God gife þe grace aganis þis gude new-ȝeir.   56

<small>Chide wicked pastors who live unchaste lives.</small>

Bot wyte the wickit pastouris wald nocht mend;   57
Thair vitious leving all þe warld prescryvis,
Thaj tuke na tent þair traik sould turne till end,
Thaj wer so proud in þair prerogatyvis;

Ane New Yeir Gift to the Quene Mary.

For wantonnes thay wald nocht wed na wyvis, 61
Nor ȝit leif chaste, bot chop and change þair cheir:
Now, to reforme þair fylthy licherous lyvis,
God gife þe grace aganis þis guid new ȝeir. 64

Thaj brocht þair bastardis, with þe skrufe thaj skraip — They have married their bastards into noble families, and have bought pardons for their sins from the Pope.
To blande þair blude with barrownis, be ambitioun!
Thaj purchest pithles pardonis fra þe paip,
To caus fond folis confyde he hes fruitioun
As god, to gif for synnis full remissioun, 69
And saulis to saif frome suffering sorowis seir;
To sett asyde sic sortis of superstitioun,
God gife þe grace aganis þis gude new-ȝeir. 72

Thaj lost baith benefice and pentioun þat mareit, 73 — They refrained from marriage to keep their benefices, but seduced our maidens.
And quha eit flesch on frydayis was fyre-fangit;
It maid na miss quhat maidinnis þaj miscareit
On fasting dayis, thaj wer nocht brint nor hangit;
Licence for luchrie fra þair lord belangit 77
To gif indulgence, as the devill did leir;
To mend þat menȝe hes sa monye mangit, — Make them amend their ways.
God gife þe grace aganis þis guide new-ȝeir. 80

Thaj lute thy liegis pray to stokkis and stanes 81 — They taught thy people to pray to stocks and stones and painted papers, and to worship relics to save their kindred's souls.
And paintit paiparis, wattis nocht quhat þaj meine;
Thaj bad þame bek and bynge at deid mennis banes;
Offer on kneis to kiss, syne saif þair kin:
Pilgrimes and palmaris past with þame betuene, 85
Sanct Blais, Sanct Boit, blait bodeis ein to bleir:
Now to forbid þis grit abuse, hes bene, — Forbid these abuses.
God gife þe grace aganis þis guid new-ȝeir. 88

Thaj tyrit god with tryfillis, tvme trentalis, 89 — They tired God with their trentals, diriges, and obits,
And daifit him with daylie dargeis,
With owklie abitis, to augment þair rentalis,
Mantand mort-mvmlingis, mixt with monye leis.
Sic sanctitude was sathanis sorcereis 93
Christis sillie scheip and sobir flok to smeir: — and misled Christ's flock.
To ceiss all sindrye sectis of hereseis,
God gif þe grace aganis þis guid new-ȝeir. 96

6   *Ane New Yeir Gift to the Quene Mary.*   [1.

[lf. 91, p. 243]
I shall not meddle with the mass; it is too deep for me.

    With mess nor matynes nowayis will I mell,   97
To iuge þame iustlie passis my ingyne;
Thaj gyde nocht ill that governis weill þame sell
And lelalie on lawtie layis þair lyne:
Dowtis to discus for doctouris, ar devyne   101
Cunnyng in clergie to declair þame cleir:
To ordour this, the office now is thyne,
God gife þe grace aganis þis gude new-ȝeir.   104

The faithful take instruction from God's word as bees take honey from the flowers.

    As beis takkis walx and honye of the floure,   105
So dois þe faythfull of goddis word tak frute;
As waspis ressauis of þe same bot soure,
So reprobatis christis buke dois rebute:
Wordis without werkis availȝeis nocht a cute: 109
To seiss thy subiectis so in lufe and feir,

See that justice and reason take root in thy kingdom.

That rycht and reasoun in thy realme may rute,
God gife þe grace aganis þis gude new-ȝeir.   112

The epistles and gospels are preached,

    The epistollis and evangelis now ar prechit,   113
But sophistrie or ceremoneis vaine;

idolatry is denounced,

Thy pepill, maist pairt, trewlie now ar techit
To put away idolatrie prophaine:

but covetousness is springing up in some hearts—Root it out!

Bot in sum hartis is gravit new agane,   117
Ane image callit Cuvatyce of Geir:
Now, to expell þat idoll, standis vp plane,
God gif þe grace aganis þis gude new-ȝeir.   120

Some go to church and sing psalms,

    For sum, ar sene at sermonis, seme sa halye,   121
Singand Sanct Dauidis psalter on þair bukis,

but they are hypocrites and think only of their bellies, they are backbiters, and rack renters.

And ar bot biblistis fairsing full þair bellie,
Bakbytand nychtbouris noyand þame in nwikis,
Ruging and raifand vp kirk rentis lyke ruikis;   125
As werrie waspis aganis goddis word makis weir:
Sic christianis to kis with chanteris kuikis,
God gife þe grace aganis þis gude new-ȝeir.   128

Debts are increased by cunning,

    Dewtie and dettis ar drevin by dowbilnes,   129
Auld folkis ar flemit fra ȝung fayth professouris;
The grittest ay, the grediar I gess
To plant quhair preistis and personis wer possessouris,

1.] *Ane New Yeir Gift to the Quene Mary.* 7

Teindis ar vptane be testament transgressouris, 133   teinds [tithes] are raised.
Credence is past off promeiss, thocht thaj sweir:
To punisch papistis and reproche oppressouris,   Punish papists,
God gif þe grace aganis þis gude new-3eir. 136   reprove oppressors.

Pure folk ar famist with thir fassionis new, 137   The poor are famishing,
Thaj faill for falt þat had befoir at fouth
Leill labouraris lamentis and tennentis trew,   loyal labourers and honest farmers are injured and driven from their homes.
That þaj ar hurt and hareit north and south:
The heidismen hes 'cor mundum' in þair mouth, 141
Bot nevir with mynd to gif þe man his meir;
To quenche thir quent calamiteis so cowth,   Right their wrongs!
God gife þe grace aganis þis gude new-3eir. 144

Protestandis takis þe freiris auld antetewme, 145   The Protestants are like the Friars, they take all they can get. The landlords raise rents, [leaf 91 b, p. 244] and ask for the help of your officers to seize their tenants' cattle.
Reddie ressauaris, bot to rander nocht;
So lairdis vpliftis mennis leifing ouir thy rewme,
And ar rycht crabit quhen thay crave þame ocht;
Be thaj vnpayit, thy pursevandis ar socht, 149
To pund pure communis corne and cattell keir:
To wisy all þir wrangus workis, ar wrocht,
God gife þe grace aganis þis gude new-3eir. 152

Paull biddis nocht deill with thingis idolatheit, 153   Paul condemns idolatry and hypocrisy. The property of the clergy is coveted by the laymen;
Nor quhair hypocrasie hes bene committit,
Bot kirk-mennis cursit substance semis sweit
Till land-men, with þat leud burd-lyme ar lyttit;
Giff thow persave sum sen3eour, it hes smittit, 157
Solist þame softlie nocht to perseveir: bid them hands off.
Hurt nocht þair honour, thocht thy hienes witt it
Bot graciouslie forgife þame þis gude 3eir. 160

Foirgifanis grant, with glaidnes and gude will, 161   Grant pardon to all:
Gratis till all into 3our parliament;
Syne stabill statutis, steidfast to stand still,
That barrone, clerk, and burges be content.   make nobles, clergy, and burgesses content.
Thy nobillis, erlis, and lordis consequent 165
Treit tendir, to obtene þair hartis inteir;
That þaj may serve and be obedient
Vnto thy grace, aganis þis gude new 3eir. 168

Ane New Yeir Gift to the Quene Mary. [1.

Make all
classes attend
to their own
business,

Sen so thow sittis in saitt superlatywe, 169
Caus everye stait to þair vocatioun go,
Scolastik men þe scriptouris to descrywe,
And maiestratis to vse þe swerd also,
Merchandis to trafique, and travell to and fro 173
Mechanikis wirk, husbandis to saw and scheir;

and wealth
will increase.

So sal be welth, and weilfaire without wo
Be grace of God aganis þis guid new ȝeir. 176

Let the land
prepare

Latt all thy realme be now in reddines, 177
With coistlie clething to decoir thy corss;
Ȝung gentilmen for dansing þame address,
With courtlie ladyes cuplit in consorss;

for your wed-
ding this
year.

Frak ferce gallandis for feild gemmis enforss; 181
Enarmit knychtis at listis with scheild and speir,
To fecht in barrowis bayth on fute and horss,
Agane thy grace gett ane guidman þis ȝeir. 184

Ambassadors
from princes
and kings
will arrive
with offers
of marriage.

This ȝeir sal be imbassatis heir belyffe 185
For mariage, frome princes, dukis, and kingis;
This ȝeir, within thy regioun, sall aryfe,
Rowtis of the rankest þat in Europ ringis;
This ȝeir bayth blythnes, and abundance bringis 189
Naveis of schippis, outthrocht the sea to sneir,
With riches, raymentis, and all royall thingis,
Agane thy grace get ane gudeman þis ȝeir. 192

If old saws
be true the
person that
shall possess
all Britain

Giffe sawis be suth to schaw thy celsitude, 193
Quhat berne sould bruke all bretane be þe see?
The prophecie expreslie dois conclude—
" The frensch wyfe of the brucis blude suld be":
Thow art be lyne, fra him the nynte degree, 197
And wes king frances pairty, maik, and peir;

shall spring
from thee.

So be discente, þe same sowld spring of þe,
By grace of god agane this gude new ȝeir. 200

Cast thyself
on Christ;
cherish thy
people,
[lf. 92, p. 245]
He will lend
thee children,

Schortlie to concluid, on christ cast thy confort, 201
And chereis þame, þat thou hes vnder charge;
Suppone maist sure he sall þe send support,
And len þe lustie liberos at large:

Ane New Yeir Gift to the Quene Mary.

Beleif þat lord may harbary so thy bairge, 205
To mak braid britane blyth as bird on breir,
And þe extoll with his triumphand targe,
Wictoriuslie agane þis guid new ȝeir. 208

and harbour so thy barge as to make broad Britain glad.

L'envoy.

Prudent, maist gent, tak tent, and prent þe wordis
Intill this bill, with will thame still to face 210
Quhilkis ar nocht skar to bar on far fra bowrdis[1]
Bot leale, but feale; may haell avaell thy grace!
Sen lo, thow scho, þis to now do, hes place, 213
Resaif swaif, and haif ingraif it heir:
This now, for prow, þat pow, sweit dow, may brace,
Lang space, with grace, solace, and peace, þis ȝeir. 216

[1 MS. 'bawrdis']

Lectori.

Fresch, fulgent, flurist, fragrant flour formois, 217
Lantern to lufe, of ladeis lamp and lot,
Cherie maist chaist, cheif charbucle and chois;
Smaill sweit smaragde, smelling but smit of smot:
Noblest natour, nurice to nurtour; not[e] 221
This dull indyte, dulce dowble dasy deir,
Send be thy sempill servand Sanderris Scott:
Greting grit god to grant thy grace gude ȝeir. 224

2.

[leaf 130, p. 319]

The iusting and debait by at the Drum, Betuix Mr Adamsone, and Johnie Sym.

A lady was the cause of the tournament.

The grit debait and turnament,
Off trewth no toung can tell,
Wes for a lusty lady gent,
Betuix twa freikis fell ;   4
For mars the god armipotent
Was no*ch*t sa ferss himsell,
Nor hercules, that aikkis vprent
And dang the devill of hell / wi*th* hornis ;   8
    Vp at the Drum that day.

The twelve peers [of Charlemagne] did not do such doughty deeds as these two knights.

Doutles wes no*ch*t so duchty deidis   10
Amangis the dowsy peiris,
Nor ʒit no clerk in story reid*is*
Off sa tryvmphand weir*is* ;   13
To se so stowtly on their steid*is*
Tha stalwart knychtis steir*is*
Quhill bellyis bair for brodding bleid*is*
With spurris als scherp as breir*is* / and kene ;
    Vp at the Drum that day.

Neither would yield, so the day and place of battle were named.

Vp at the Drum the day wes sett   19
And fixt wes þe feild,
Quhair baith thir noble chiftanis mett
Enarmit vndir scheild ;   22
Thay wer sa haisty and sa hett,
That nane of thame wald ʒeild,
Bot to debait, or be doun bett
And in the quarrell keild / or slane ;   26
    Vp at the Drum þat day.

Thair wes ane bettir and ane worss 28 *Of the two William was the heavier,*
I wald þat it wer wittin,
For William wichttar wes of corss
Nor Sym, and bettir knittin. 31
Sym said he sett no*ch*t by his forss
Bot hecht he sowld be hittin,
And he micht counter Will on horss,
For sym wes bettir sittin / nor Will; 35 *but Sym sat better on horseback.*
    Vp at the Drum that day.

To se the stryfe come ȝunkeirs stowt, 37 *Many came to see the fight.*
And mony galȝart ma*n*;
All denteis deir wes thair but dowt,
The wyne on broich it ran: 40
Trumpettis and schalmis w*ith* a schowt *The trumpets sounded,*
Playid or the rink began;
And eikwall juges satt abowt *and the judges took*
To se quha tynt or wan / the feild; 44 *their seats.*
    Vp at the Drum that day.

W*ith* twa blunt trincher speiris squair, 46 *[leaf 130 b, p. 320]*
It wes thair interpryiss *They were to fight with*
To fecht, w*ith* baith thair facis bair, *spears,*
For lufe, as is the gyiss: 49
Ane freynd of thair*is* throw hap come thair,
And hard the rumor ryiss;
Quha stall away thair styngis bath clair, *but some one hid the*
And hid in secreit wayiss / For skaith; 53 *weapons.*
    Vp at [the Drum that day].

Strang me*n* of armes and of micht, 55
Wer sett thame for to sidder;
The harrald*is* cryd, "God schaw the rycht," *The heralds cried, "God,*
Syne bad thame go togidder. 58 *show the right," and bade them*
"Quhair is my speir?" sayis sym the knycht, *fight.*
"Sum ma*n* go bring it hidder;" *Sym asked for his spear,*
But wald they tary thair all nycht,
Thair lanciss come to lidder / & slaw; 62 *but it could not be found.*
    Vp at [the Drum that day].

He jumped from his horse,	Sym flew als fery as a fowne,	64
	Doun fra the horss he slaid,	
cursing the hider.	Sayis, "he sall rew my stalf hes stowin,	
	For I sal be his deid."	67
William vowed to the peacock.	William his vow plicht to the powin	
	For favour or for feid,	
	"Als gude the tre had nevir growin,	
	Quhairof my speir wes maid / to just";	71
	Vp at [the Drum that day].	
The two knights retired to eat,	Thĩr vowis maid to syn and mone,	73
	They raikit baith to rest,	
	Thame to refress with thair disione,	
	And of thair armour kest,	76
	Nocht knawing of the deid wes done;	
but they found the fire that was to cook their food had been put out.	Quhen thay suld haif fairin best,	
	The fyre wes pischt out lang or none,	
	Thair dennaris suld haif drest / and dicht;	80
	Vp at [the Drum that day].	
Enraged at being fooled they swore vengeance,	Than wer thay movit owt of mynd,	82
	Far mair than of beforne;	
	Thay wist nocht how to get him pynd,	
	That thame had drevin to skorne.	85
	Thair wes no deth mycht be devynd,	
and said the culprit should dearly pay for his work.	But ethis haif thay sworne,	
	He suld deir by, be thay had dynd,	
	And ban that he was borne, / or bred;	89
	Vp at the Drum þat day.	
[leaf 131, p. 321] They go on to Dalkeith where there is great feasting;	Than to Dalkeith thai maid thame boun,	91
	Reidwod of this reproche;	
	Thair wes baith wyne and vennisoun,	
	And barrellis ran on broche:	94
and made a compact not to separate.	They band vp kyndnes in that toun,	
	Nane fra his feir to foche,	
	For thair wes nowdir lad nor loun	
	Mycht eit ane baikin-loche / For fowness;	98
	Vp at Dalkeith þat day.	

The justing and debait vp at the Drum.

Syne eftir denner raiss the din, 100 *After dinner Sym incites William,*
And all the toun on steir :
William wes wyiss, and held him in,
For he wes in a feir ; 103
Sym to haif bargan cowld no*ch*t blin,
Bot bukkit Will on weir,
Sayis, " gife thow wald this lady win,
Cum furth and brek a speir / w*ith* me "; 107
    Vp at Dalkeyt*h* þat day.

This still for bargan Sym abyddis, 109 *and tries to shame him into a fight.*
And schowttit Will to schame ;
Will saw his fais on baith the syddis,
Full fair he dred for blame : 112
Will schortly to his horss he slydis,   *Will answers that they would be better employed buying hides at home than in what they are doing.*
And sayis to Sym be name,
" Bettir we bath wer byand hyddis
" And weddir sky*n*nis at hame / nor heir"; 116
    Vp at [Dalkeith þat day].

Now is the growme that wes so grym 118
Rycht glaid to leif in lie :
" Fy, theif, for schame," sayis littill Sym,   *Sym chides Will,*
" Will thow no*ch*t fecht w*ith* me ? 121
" Thow art moir lerge of lyth and lym,
" Nor I am, be sic thre,"
And all the feild cryd, fy on him !   *and the people mock at him.*
Sa cowartly tuk the fle / for feir ; 125
    Vp at [Dalkeith that day].

Than every ma*n* gaif Will a mok, 127
And said, he wes our meik :
Sayis Sym, " send for thy broder Jok,   *Sym asks Will to send for his brother, and says he would fight both of them, even if he had only a distaff.*
" I sall no*ch*t be to seik ; 130
" For wer ȝe foursum in a flok,
" I compt ȝow no*ch*t a leik,
" Tho*ch*t I had rycht no*ch*t but a rok
" To gar ȝour rumpill reik / behynd," 134   [leaf 131 *b*, p. 322]
    Vp at Dalkeith þat day.

	Thair wes richt no*ch*t bot haif and ga,	136
	W*ith* law*ch*ter lowd thay lewche,	
	Quhen they saw sym sic curage ta,	
	And will mak it sa twche :	139
	Sym lap on horsback lyk a ra,	
	And ran him till a huche,	
Sym challanges Will to ride down a steep brae,	Sayis " William, cum ryde doun this bra,	
	Tho*ch*t ʒe suld brek ane bwche / Fo[r] lufe "	143
	Vp at [Dalkeith this day].	

and then gallops down himself;	Sone doun the bra Sym braid lyk thunder,	145
	And bad Will fallow fast ;	
	To grund, for fersness, he did funder,	
half way down Sym's horse stumbled.	Be he midhill had past.	148
	William saw Sym in sic a blunder,	
	To ga he wes agast ;	
Will is too afraid to follow.	For he affeird, it wes na winder	
	His cursour suld him cast / and hurt him,	152
	Vp [at Dalkeith that day].	

The people call on Will to yield.	Than all the ʒungkeiris bad Will ʒeild,	154
	Or doun the glen to gang ;	
	Sum cryd " the koward suld be keild ; "	
	Sum doun the hewche he thrang ;	157
	Sum ruscht, sum ru*m*myld, [and] sum reild ;	
	Sum be the bewche he hang ;	
	Thair avairis fyld vp all the feild,	
	They wer sa fow and pang, / w*ith* drafe	161
	Vp [at Dalkeith that day].	

John comes into the field armed with sword and buckler.	Than gelly Johine come in a jak	163
	To feild quhair he wes feidit,	
	Abone his brand ane bucklar blak,	
Woe befall the man who feels his brand. He rides down the hill.	Baill fell the bern thad bed it ;	166
	He slippit swiftly to the slak,	
	And rudly doun he raid it ;	
	Befoir his curpall wes a crak	169
	Culd na man tell quha maid it / For law*ch*tter	
	Vp at [Dalkeith that day].	

2.]   *The justing and debait vp at the Drum.*   15

  Be than the bowgill gan to blaw,   172   It gets dark;
  For nycht had thame ourtane;   after the bugle has sounded
  " Allaiss," said sym, " for falt of law,
  That bargan get I nane."   175
  Thuss hame wit*h* mony crak & flaw   they go homewards,
  Thay passid every ane;   and part at Potterow
  Syne pairtit at the Potter-raw,   Port.
  And sindry gaitis ar gane / to rest thame   179
    Wit*h*in the toun þat nycht.

     L'envoy.   [leaf 132, p. 323]
  This Will was he, begyld the may,   181   Will was the man who
  And did hir m*e*rriage spill;   beguiled the girl, and
  He promeist hir, to lat him play,   spoiled her marriage,
  Hir purpos to fulfill;   184
  Fra scho fell fow, he fled away,   and then left her in the
  And come na mair hir till;   lurch.
  Quhairfoir he tynt the feild that day,   This was why he had to run
  And tuk him to ane mill, / to hyd him   188   away and hide himself.
    As coward fals of fey.

3.
Of May.

<table>
<tr><td>[leaf 156 b, p. 372]

May is the month for those in the service of Venus.</td><td>May is the moneth maist amene
For thame in Venus *scher*uice bene,
To recreat thair havy hartis:
May caussis curage frome the splene,
And every thing in May revartis.</td><td>1

5</td></tr>
<tr><td>The trees bud, the blackbirds sing; the maidens play with tabors and at upcoil.</td><td>In May the pleasant spray vpspringis;
In May the mirthfull maveiss singis;
And now in May to mady*n*nis fawis,
With tymmer wechtis to trip in ringis,
And to play vpcoill w*ith* the bawis.</td><td>6

10</td></tr>
<tr><td>The gallants play music.</td><td>In May gois gallandis bring in sy*m*mer,
And trymly occupyis thair ty*m*mer,
With " Hunts vp " every mor*n*ing plaid.</td><td>11</td></tr>
<tr><td>Women dress more gaily to gladden their lovers.</td><td>In May gois gentill wemen gymmer,
In gardy*n*nis grene thair gru*m*is to glaid.</td><td>
15</td></tr>
<tr><td>In old times people used to perform in May, Robin Hood and Little John and the</td><td>In May quhe*n* men ȝeid everichone,
W*ith* Robene Hoid and Littill Johne,
To bring in bowis and birkin bobbynis:
Now all sic game is fastlingis gone
Bot gif it be amangis clown robbynis.</td><td>16

20</td></tr>
<tr><td>Abbot of Unreason.</td><td>Abbotis by rewll, and lord*is* but ressone,
Sic senȝeo*uris* tymis ourweill this sessone;
Vpoun thair vyce war lang to waik,
Quhais falsatt, fibilnes and tressone,
Hes rung thryis oure this zodiak.</td><td>21

25</td></tr>
<tr><td>The cuckoo begins to sing in May.</td><td>In May begy*n*nis the golk to gaill;
In May drawis deir to doun and daill;
In May men mellis with famyny,
And ladeis meitis thair luvaris laill
Quhen Phebus is in Gemyny.</td><td>26

30</td></tr>
</table>

Butter, new-cheis, and beir in May, 31   New dishes come in. [leaf 157, p. 373]
Cōmamis, cokkillis, curd*is* and quhay,
Lapstaris, lempettis, mussillis in schellis,
Grene leikis, and all sic me*n* may say,
Suppois sum of thame sourly smellis. 35

In May grit men w*ith*in thair bound*is*, 36   Noblemen go out with hawks and hounds,
Sum halk*is* the walteris, sum w*ith* houn*dis*
The hairis owt-throwch the forrestis cachis,
Syne efter thame thair ladeis found*is*,   and the ladies follow after.
To sent the rynnyng of the rachis. 40

In May frank archeris will affix 41   Archers go shooting.
In place to meit: syne marrowis mix,
To schute at buttis at bankis & brais;
Sum at the reveris, sum at the prikkis;
Sum laich and to beneth the clais. 45

In May sowld me*n* of amour*is* go, 46   Men should wait on their lady loves.
To serf thair ladeis, and no mo,
Sen thair releis in ladeis lyis;
For sum may cum in favo*uris* so,
To kiss his loif on buchone wyis. 50

In may gois da*m*mosalis and da*m*mis 51   Damsels and dames go out in the gardens for games.
In gardyngis¹ grene to play lyk la*m*mis;
Sum at the bairis thay brace lyk billeis;
Sum ry*n*nis at barlabreikis lyk ra*m*mis,
Sum round abowt the standand pilleis. 55

In May gois madynis till Lareit, 56   The maidens visit Loretto.
And hes thair myn3onis on the streit,
To horss thame quhair the gait is ruch:
Sum at Inche-bukling-bray they meit,
Sum in the midd*is* of Mussilburch. 60

So May and all thir monethis thre, 61
Are hett and dry in thair degre;
Heirfoir 3e wantoun men in 3owth,
For helth of body now haif E,   For health's sake
No*ch*t oft till mell w*ith* thankless mowth. 65

¹ MS. reads "gardyingis."

18   *Of May.*   [4.

[leaf 157 b,   Sen every pastyme is at plesure,   66
  p. 374]   I counsale ȝow to mel with mesure,
                  And namely now, May, June, & Julij,
delight not   Delyt nocht lang in luvaris lesure,
over much in
the pleasures   But weit ȝour lippis & labor hully.   70
of love.

4.

[O Lusty May, with Flora Quene.]

[leaf 229 b,   O lusty May, with flora quene,   1
  p. 518]   The balmy dropis frome Phebus schene,
Hail, lusty   Preluciand bemes befoir þe day,
May!   Be that Diana growis grene,
                  Throwch glaidnes of þis lusty May.   5

                  Than esperus, that is so bricht,   6
                  Till wofull hairtis castis his lycht,
                  With bankis that blumes on euery bray,
                  And schuris ar sched furth of þair sicht
                  Thruch glaidnes of this lusty May.   10

All nature   Birdis on bewis of every birth,   11
rejoices in   Reiosing nottis makand thair mirth,
thee,   Rycht plesandly vpoun the spray
                  With fflurissingis our feild & firth
                  Thruch [glaidnes of thus lusty May].   15

                  All luvaris that ar in cair   16
                  To thair ladeis thay do repair,
                  In fresch mornyngis befoir the day,
                  And ar in mirth ay mair and mair,
                  Thruch glaidnes of this lusty May.   20

the gayest   [1][Of every moneth in the year,   21
month of the   To mirthful May there is no peer;
year.   Her glistring garments are so gay,
                  Your Lovers all, make merry cheer,
                  Through gladness of this lusty May.]   25

[1] *Cantus, Songs and Fancies.* I. Forbes, Aberdeen, 1682, leaf 11.

Poems on the Pains and Pleasures of Love.

5.

[Luve preysis but comparesone.]

Luve preysis, but comparesone,	1	[leaf 213 b, 486]
Both gentill, sempill, generall;		Love conquers gentle and simple,
And of fre will gevis waresone,		
As fortoun chansis to befall:		
For luve makis nobill ladeis thrall,	5	and makes the noble the thrall of the base born.
To bassir men of birth and blud;		
So luve garris sobir wemen small,		
Get maistrice our grit men of gud.	8	
Ferme luve, for fauour, feir, or feid,	9	
Of riche nor pur to speik suld spair;		
For luve to hienes hes no heid,		
Nor lychtleis lawlines ane air;		
But puttis all personis in compair,	13	Love puts all on an equality.
This prowerb planely for till preue,		
That men and wemen, less and mair,		
Ar cumd of Adame and of Eue.	16	
So thocht my lyking wer a leddy,	17	Though I were of low degree and my love of high, my service would be as good as a duke's.
And I no lord, ȝit nocht þe less		
Scho suld my serwyce find als reddy		
As duke to duches docht him dress;		
For as prowd princely luve express	21	
Is to haif souerenitie;		
So serwice cumis of sympilness,		
And leilest lufe of law degre.	24	

20　　　　*Haif hairt in hairt, ȝe hairt of hairtis, haill.*　[6.

<small>Therefore no man should lack the art of love.</small>

 So luvaris lair no leid suld lak;　　　25
 A lord to lufe a silly lass,
 A leddy als for luf to tak
 Ane prope*r* page hir tyme to pass:
 For quhy as bricht bene birneist brass　　29
 As siluer wrocht at all dewyss;
 And als gud drinking out of glass
 As gold, tho*ch*t gold gif grittar pryss.　　32

<small>Should I show these verses?

No! I am afraid she will be displeased.</small>

 Suld I presome þis sedull schaw,　　33
 Or lat me langouris be lamentit?
 Na! I effrey for feir and aw,
 Hir comlie heid be miscontenttit.
 I dar no*ch*t preiss hir to present it;　　37
 For be scho wreth I will no*ch*t wow it,
 But pleiss hir prowdens to impre*n*t it,
 Scho may persaue sum inglis throw it.　　40

6.

[Haif hairt in hairt, ȝe hairt of hairtis, haill.]

<small>[leaf 228, p. 515]

Sweetheart, have my heart,</small>

 Haif hairt in hairt, ȝe hairt of hairtis, haill;　1
 Trewly sweit hairt, ȝour hairt my hairt sal haif;
 Expell deir hairt my havy hairtis baill;
 Praying ȝow hairt quhilk hes my hairt in graif,
 Sen ȝe sweit hairt, my hairt may sla & saif,　5

<small>let it not be lost.</small>

 Lat nocht deir hairt my leill hairt be forloir,
 Excelland hairt, of every hairtis gloir.　7

<small>My heart is glad to serve you;</small>

 Glaid is my hairt, with ȝow sueit hairt to rest,　8
 And serue ȝow hairt, with hairtis observance;
 Sen ȝe ar, hairt, with bayth our hairtis possest,
 My hairt is in ȝour hairtis gouernance;

<small>do with it as you will,</small>

 Do with my hairt, ȝour hairtis sweit plesance,　12
 For is my hairt thrall ȝour hairt vntill;
 I haif no hairt contrair ȝour hairtis will.　14

The ansueir to the ballat of hairtis.

Sen ȝe haif hairt, my faythfull hairt, in cure, 15
Vphald þe hairt, quhilk is ȝour hairtis awin ;
Gif my hairt be ȝour hairtis scheruiture,
How may ȝe thoill ȝour trew hairt be ourthrawin ?
Quhairfoir sweit hairt nocht suffer so be knawin, 19
Bot ȝe be, hairt, my hairtis reiosing,   and be my heart's re-
As ȝe ar hairt of hairtis conforting.   21 joicing.

[Anon.]

7.

The anschir to the ballat of hairtis.   [leaf 235 b, p. 526]

Considdir, hairt, my trew intent,   1 Though I fail in eloquence,
Suppois I am nocht eloquent   consider my kindly inten-
  To wryt ȝow anschir responsyve ;   tention,
ȝour scedull is so excellent,
  It passis far my wyttis fyve.   5

For quhy it is so full of hairtis   6
That myne within my bosum stairtis,
  Quhen I behald it rycht till end ;
And for ilk hairt, ane hundreth dertis
  Outthrow my hairt, to ȝow I send.   10

This woundit hairt, sweit hairt, ressaif,   11 Receive this wounded heart,
Quhilk is deir hairt abone þe laif
  ȝour faythfull hairt, with trew intent ;   [leaf 236, p. 527]
Ane trewar hairt may no man haif,
  Nor ȝit ane hairt moir permanent.   15

Ane hairt it is without dissait ;   16 'tis free from deceit,
It is þe hairt to quhome ȝe wret
  The misseif full of hairtis seir ;
It is ane hairt bayth air & lait
  That is ȝour hairtis presoneir.   20

It is ane hairt, full of distres ;   21
Ane cairfull hairt all confortles ;   but sad, comfortless,
  Ane penseve hairt in dule & dolour,
Ane hairt of wo & haviness ;   and woful,
  Ane mirthles hairt without mesour.   25

22 *Hence, hairt, with hir þat mvst departe.* [8.

	It is ane hairt bay*th* firme & stabill 26
	Ane hairt wi*th*out fenȝeit fabill;
though constant.	Ane co*n*sta*n*t hairt bayth trest & trew;
	Ane sure hairt set in to sabill;
	Ane wofull hairt bot gif ȝe rew. 30

It is ane hairt þat ȝo*ur* hairt servis; 31
Ane hairt for lufe of ȝour hairt stervis;
It dies for your sake, though it has never offended you. Ane hairt þat nevir ȝow offendit;
Ane hairt of ȝo*uris* bayth vane & nervis;
Ane hairt but solace bot gif ȝe send it. 35

It is na gravit hairt in stone, 36
In siluer, gold, nor evir bone;
Nor ȝit ane payntit symlitud;
It is a living heart of flesh and blood. Bot this same verry hairt allone,
Wi*th*in my breist of flesch and blude. 40

Thairfoir, sueit hairt, send me þe hairt 41
That is in to ȝour breist inwart;
And no*ch*t thir writtin hairtis in vane;
Let us exchange our hearts. Bot ȝour hairt to my hairt rewert,
And send me hairt for hairt agane. 45

8.

[𝕳ence, 𝖍airt, 𝖜it𝖍 𝖍ir 𝖕at m𝖔st 𝖉eparte.]

[leaf 235, p. 525]
Hence, heart, to thy sovereign lady,
    Hence, hairt, wi*th* hir þat most depa*r*te, 1
    And hald the wi*th* thy souerane;
    For I had lever want ane harte,
    Nor haif the hairt þat dois me pane:
    Thairfoir, go, wi*th* thy lufe remane, 5
    And lat me leif thus vnmolest,
and abide with her thou lovest best,
    And se þat thow cum no*ch*t agane,
    Bot byd wi*th* hir thow luvis best. 8

[leaf 335 *b*, p. 526]
who hast departed
    Sen scho, that I haif s*ch*eruit lang, 9
    Is to depairt so suddanly;
    Address the now, for thow sall gang
    And beir thy lady cu*m*pany:

Fra scho be gon, hairtless am I;	13
For quhy thow art w*ith* hir possest;	
Thairfoir my hairt! go hence in hy,	in haste.
And byd w*ith* hir thow luvis best.	16

Thoc*h*t this belappit body heir	17	Though my body is in servitude,
Be bound to sc*h*eruitude and thrall,		
My fathfull hairt is fre inteir,		my heart is free,
And mynd to serf my lady at all:		
Wald god þat I wer perigall	21	
Vnder þat redolent ross to rest!		
Ʒit at þe leist, my hairt thow sall		and it shall serve her.
Abyd w*ith* hir thow lufis best.	24	

Sen in ʒour garth þe lilly quhyte	25	The lily must fade,
May noc*h*t remane amang þe laif,		
Adew! þe flour of haill delyte,		
Adew! þe succour þat ma me saif,		
Adew! þe fragrant balme suaif,	29	
And lamp of ladeis lustiest		
My fayt*h*full hairt scho sall it haif,		but my faithful heart
To byd w*ith* hir it luvis best.	32	shall still be true.

Deploir, ʒe ladeis cleir of hew	33	Deplore the loss,
Hir absence, sen scho most depa*r*te,		
And specialy ʒe luvaris trew		ye lovers,
That woundit bene w*ith* luvis darte:		
For su*m* of ʒow sall wa*n*t ane harte	37	for you may be left as I.
Alsweill as I; þairfoir at last		
Do go w*ith* myn, w*ith* mynd inwart,		
And byd w*ith* hir thow luvis best.	40	

9.

[Quha is perfyte to put in wryt.]

Quha is p*er*fyte / to put in wryt		[leaf 236, p. 527]
The inwart murny*ng* & mischance;		Who can write of loves' pains and pleasures?
Or to indyte / þe grit delyte	3	
Of lustie lufis obsc*h*erwance?		
Bot he þat may certa*n*e / pacie*n*tly suffir pane /		
To wyn his souerane / in reco*m*pance.	6	

24   *Quha is perfyte to put in wryt.*   [9.

I have experienced both.

  Albeid I knaw / of luvis law
  The plesour & the panis smart;
  ȝit I stand aw / for to furthschaw   9
  The quyet secreitis of my harte:

[leaf 236 b, p. 528]

For it may fortoun raith / to do hir body skaith /
Quhilk wait þat of þame baith / I am expert.   12

  S[c]ho wait my wo / that is ago,
  Scho wait my weilfair and remeid,

My lady knows I am her loyal lover.

  Scho wait also / I lufe no mo   15
  Bot hir the well of womanheid:
Scho wait withouttin faill / I am hir luvar laill /
Scho hes my hairt alhaill / till I be deid.   18

  That bird of bliss / in bewty is,
  In erd þe only a per se,
  Quhais mowth to kiss / is worth, I wiss,   21
  The warld full of gold to me:

My only care is to please her.

Is nocht in erd I cure, / bot pleiss my lady pure /
Syne be hir scheruiture / vnto I de.   24

  Scho hes[1] my lufe / at hir behufe;

My heart is hers,

  My hairt is subiect, bound, & thrall;
  For scho dois moif / my hairt aboif, | 27
  To se hir proper persoun small:
Sen scho is wrocht at will / that natur may fulfill /

and my body too.

Glaidly I gif hir till / body and all.   30

  Thair is nocht wie[2] / can estimie
  My sorrow and my sichingis sair;

Love's labours have made me sorrowful.

  For I am so / done fathfullie   33
  In fawouris with my lady fair,
That baith our hartis ar ane / luknyt in luvis chene /
And evirilk greif is gane / for evir mair.   36

---

[1] Originally "is" in MS.; altered in a later hand to "hes."
[2] Originally "wicht" in MS.; altered in same hand to "wie."

10.

[𝔍 wil be plane and lufe affane.]

I wil be plane / and lufe affane
  For as I mene / so tak me;
Gif I refrane / for wo, or pane
  ȝour lufe certane / foirsaik me.   4

Gif trew report / to ȝow resort
  Of my gud port / so tak me;
Gif I exort / in evill sort
  Without confort / forsak me.   8

Gif diligens / in ȝour presens
  Schaw my pretens / so tak me;
Gif negligens / in my absens
  Schaw my offens / forsaik me.   12

ȝouris and no mo / quhair evir I go
  Gif I so do / so tak me
Gif I fle fro / & dois nocht so
  Evin as ȝour fo / forsaik me.   16

Gif I do prufe / þat I ȝow luf
  Nixt god abufe / so taik me,
Gif I remufe / fra ȝour behufe
  Without excuss / foirsaik me.   20

Be land or se / quhair evir I be
  As ȝe fynd me / so tak me;
And gif I le / & from ȝow fle
  Ay quhill I de / forsaik me.   24

It is bot waist / mo wordis to taist
  ȝe haif my laist / so tak me
Gif ȝe our cast / my lyf is past
  Ewin at þe last / forsaik me.   28

My deir, adew / most cleir of hew
  Now on me rew / & so tak me;
Gif I persew / & beis nocht trew
  Cheiss ȝe ane new / & forsaik me.   32

11.

[Only to ȝow in erd that I lufe best.]

[leaf 237 b, p. 530]
I commend myself to you whom I love, best.

Only to ȝow in erd that I lufe best, 1
I me commend ane hundreth thowsand syiss;
Exorting ȝow, with pensyfe hairt opprest,
As ȝe ar scho quhom in my confort lyiss,
Gif I misvse my pen, or done dispyss 5
Ocht at this tyme, will God I sall amend,
Protesting this ballat ȝe attend. 7

Some lovers delight in graceful speech;

Sum luvaris thame delytis till indyte 8
Fair facound speich, blandit with eloquence;
And vþir sum dois sett þair wit perfyte
To pleiss þair ladeis with all þair diligens,

others, through want of it, fail to win their ladies.

Sum luffaris wantis, throw þair negligens, 12
For falt of speich, the lufe of his maistres,
Without hir witting [he is] in distress. 14

As to my parte, my lusty lady schene, 15

I feel such great distress

Throw laik of speich, I thoill rycht grit distress;
Bayth nycht & day, hard persit to þe splene
With deidly dert, and can find no redress;

that I must declare it

This me behuffis my panis to express; 19
Or than, knaw rycht weill, but wirdis moir,
That crewell dert out[t]hrow my hart wald boir. 21

rather than smart.

Rathir nor smart / I mon my harme reweill 22
To ȝow my hairt / quha ma my baillis beit;
For & ȝe start / adew all warldly weill!
Will ȝe rewart / my cairis ar compleit.
Tuiching ȝour parte / I prey ȝow be discreit, 26

[leaf 238, p. 531] If you pity me, I shall be true until death parts us.

For eftirwart / gif ȝe vpoun me rew,
Quhill deid departe / my lyfe I sal be trew. 28

Secreit alswa / in every maner sort, 29
For weill nor wa / sall ony knaw our mynd?

Be not backward to comfort your servant.

Than be nocht thra ȝour scherwand to confort:
Sum anschir ma / as ȝe ar gud and kynd, 32
That may me, fra / my langour appeill, þat is pynd,

And not[1] sla / me throw ȝour negligence;
This I ȝow pra / for ȝour he excellens.   35

Adew / rycht trew / adew my deirest hairt;   36
Fairest of hew / for this tyme haif gud nycht;
Remord & rew / and pondir weill my pairte,
Sen I persew / na thing of ȝow bot rycht;
Quhilk gif ȝe knew / my mynd as it is plicht,   40   *If you knew my feelings you would grant my desire.*
Ȝe wald subdew / ȝour inwart thocht & mynd,
And me reskew quhilk for ȝour lufe is pynd.   42

12.
[Rycht as þe glass bene thirlit thrucht with bemis.]

Rycht as þe glass bene thirlit thrucht with bemis   1   [leaf 239 b, p. 534]
Off Phebus fair prefulgent visage bricht,
Or [as] hornit Dyane with hir paly glemis,   *As Diana's pale beams pierce the black clouds,*
Perssis the cluddis sabill in þe nicht;
And as the kocatrice keilis with hir sicht;   5
Rycht so þe bewty of my lady stoundis   *so my lady's beauty shoots into my heart.*
Out-throwcht my breist, vnto my hairt redoundis.   7

Behaild how far cristall or diamant,   8   *As a diamond*
Jassink, jasp, ruby jem, or criselleit,
Carbunkile, emmerauld, perle, or athamant,
Turcas, topas, marbill, or margareit,
Exceidis the barrat stonis in þe streit: 12   *to a common stone,*
In lykwayis dois hir bewty vndegraid,
Transcend all vþiris, wyfe, wedow, or maid.   14

Espy richt so how far þe rosy gowlis   15
Passis the wallowit weidis in þe vaill;
Or sound of lark aboif þe revenous fowlis;   *or the voice of a lark to the croak of a raven,*
And somersday the nichtis hiemaill;
Or as ane galay gayest vndir saill   19
Bene plesandar nor taikles boitis small;   *so is my love's beauty to that of other women.*
So is my lady lustiest of all.   21

[1] "not"; MS. reads "to."

13.

"Up, helsum hairt! thy rutis rais, & lowp."

[leaf 242 b, p. 540] Be joyful, my heart,	Vp, helsum hairt! thy rutis rais, and lowp; Exalt and clym within my breist in staige; Art thow nocht wantoun, haill, & in gud howp, Fermit in grace, and free of all thirlaige, Bathing in bliss, and sett in hie curaige?	1 5
thou hast won thy lady's heart.	Braisit in joy, no falt may the affray, Having thy ladeis hart as heretaige, In blenche-ferme ffor ane sallat every May: So neidis thow nocht now sussy, sytt, nor sorrow, Sen thow art sure of sollace evin & morrow.	 10
Cupid, I am thy liege,	Thow Cupeid rewardit me with thiss; I am thy awin trew liege, withowt tressone. Thair levis no man in moir eiss, welth, and bliss,	11
I know no sadness.	I knaw no siching, sadnes, nor ʒit soun, Walking, thocht, langour, lamentatioun, Dolor, dispair, weiping nor jelosye; My breist is woyd and purgit of pussoun;	15
I feel no pain.	I feill no pane, I haif no purgatorye; Bot peirles, perfytt, paradisall plesour, With mirry hairt and mirthfulnes but mesoure.	 20
	My lady, lord, thow gaif me for to hird:	21
I fondle my love,	Within myne armes I nureiss on the nycht; Kissing, I say, my bab, my tendir bird, Sweit maistres, lady luffe, & lusty wicht, Steir, rewll, and gyder of my senssis richt! My voice surmontis the sapheir cludis hie, Thanking grit god of that tressour & micht. I coft hir deir, bot scho fer derrer me,	 25
who has committed herself to my care.	Quhilk hasard honor, fame in aventeur, Committing clene hir corse to me in cure.	 30
We kiss and play and sport,	In oxsteris cloiss we kiss, and cossis hairtis, Brynt in desyre of amouris play and sport;	31
[leaf 243, p. 541]	Meittand oure lustis, spreitles we twa depairtis. Prolong with lasar, lord, I the exhort	

Sic tyme that we may boith tak our confort ;   35
First for to sleip, syne walk w*ith*owt espyis ;
I blame the cok, I plene the nicht is schort :   *and I blame*
Away I went, my wache the cuschett cryis,   *the shortness of the night.*
Wissing all luvaris leill to haif sic chance
That thay may haif ws in reme*m*brance.   40

14.
[How suld my febill body fure.]

Bannatyne MS.   *Panmure MS.*

Bannatyne MS.		Panmure MS.		
How suld my febill body fure,		Houe sould my feible bodie fure		[Bann. MS., leaf 244 b, p. 544]
The dowble dolour I indure,		The double dolor þat I indure,		
The morny*n*g and the grit mallure,		The murning & the great malure		
Ca*n* nane devyne ;	4	Can not defin ;	4	
Quhilk garris my bailfull breist com-		It dois my belful breist combure,		*My lady loves another.*
To se ane vþ*ir* haif þe cure, [bure		To see an other haue in cure		
þ*a*t suld by myne.	7	þat sould be myne.	7	
For weill I wait wes nevir wicht,	8	For veil I vat vas neuer a vight,	8	
Wald sa inforss his myn*d* & mycht,		þat culd inforce his mynd & mighte,		
To lufe & serf his lady bricht		To loue & serwe his Lady brighte		
And want hir syne,	11	& vant hir sine,	11	
As I do, martir day and nyc*h*t,		As I doe, martire day & nighte,		
W*ith*out the only thing of rycht,		Vithout þat onlie thing of right,		
That [suld be myne].	14	That sulde be mine.	14	
War I of pissans for to prufe,	15	Ver I offe pussans for to prowe,	15	*Would I could prove my loyalty.*
My lawty & my hairtly lufe,		My lautie & my hairtlie lowe,		
I suld hir mynd to me*r*cy mufe,		I suld hir mynd to mercie mowe,		
W*ith* sic propyne.	18	Vith such propyne	18	
War all þe warld at my behufe,		Var al this vorld at my behowe,		
Scho suld it haif, be god abufe,		She sould it haue, be god aboue,		
That suld be myne.	21	For to be myne.	21	
Now quhome to sall I mak my mone,		Noue quhome to sal I mak my mone,		*To whom shall I complain?*
Sen trewt*h* & co*n*sta*n*s fynd I none,		Since treuthe & constans find I none,		
For all the fathfull lufe is gone		For al the faithful loue is gone		
Of femenene.	25	Of feminine ;	25	*It would crush a heart of stone to see me lost on account of my unkind love.*
It wald vpross ane hart of stone,		It vald oppresse ane hairt of stone,		
To se me lost for lufe of one		To sie me die for hir alone		
That [suld be myne].	28	þ*a*t suld be mynne.	28	

Who can raise my spirits?	Quha suld my dullit spreitis raiss, 29
	Sen for no lufe my lady gaiss,
	Bot and gud scheruice mycht hir maiss
	    Scho suld inclyne. 32
	I dre þe dollour and diseiss,
	Quhen vþiris hes hir as thay pleiss,
	    That suld be myne. 35
		Vha sal my dullit spreits rease 29
		Since not for loue my lady gais
		For & guid seruice might hir please
		    She vald inclynne. 32
		I drie both dolor & desease,
		& others has hir as they please,
		    þat suld be mynne. 35

I may persaif þat weill be thiss 36   Now I persaue right veil be this 36
That all the blythnes, joy, and bliss, þat al the blydnes, Ioy, and blysse,
The lusty, wantoun lyfe, I wiss,   The lustie, vantone life, I vysse,
    Of lufe is hyne; 39   Of loue is hynne; 39

There is no remedy but patience.
And no remeid, sen so it iss,   Quhat remedie, since so it is,
Bot paciens, suppoiss I miss   Bot patiens, suppose I mysse
    That suld be myne. 42   þat suld be mynne. 42

For nobillis hes nocht ay renown, 43 For nobles has not ay renunne, 43
Nor gentillis ay the gayest goun,   Nor gentils ay the gayest gune;
Thay cary victuallis to þe toun   They carie vitual to the tune
    That werst dois dyne: þat varst does dynne:

Though I get to the bush, another eats the berry.
Sa bissely to busk I boun,   So bisilie to busse I bune
Ane vþir eitis the berry doun   & uthers eats the berrie doune
    That suld be myn[e]. 49   þat sould be mynne. 49

Quha wald the rege of ȝowtheid dant,
Let thame the court of luvaris hant,
And tham as Venus subiectis grant   [*Lines 50 to 56 not in Panmure*
    And keip hir tryme: 53   *MS.*]
Perchance thay sall find freindschip skant,
And abill thair reward to want,
    As I did myne. 56

15.

[Marvilling in mynd, quhat ailis fortoun at me.]

[leaf 245, p. 545]
What ails Fortune at me?

Marvilling in mynd, quhat ailis fortoun at me,
And I ane scherwand trew both day and nycht,
I am bot deid sic dolour for to dre
So suddanly exylit frome hir sycht. 4
In all this warld thair is no erdly wycht
Moir fre, moir fremmit, moir trest, & eik moir trew;
Sen I mon de, adew, luvaris, adew. 7

Marvilling in mynd, quhat ailis fortoun at me.

    Dame Natur! I the wyt of all my pane,   8 I blame
    That formit hes this flour so fair but feir,   Dame
    All vertew in hir visage dois remane,   Nature,
    Bot merciles I go from ȝeir to ȝeir;   11
    Scho is allon of price withouttin peir:
    This ryall ross will nocht vpoun me rew;   because my
    Sen I mon de, adew, luvaris, adew.   14 lady is ruth-
      less.

    My dullit hairt but dout may nocht indure,   15
    My pane but peir, it perssis throw my hairt;
    My lady fair, of me scho takis no cure,
    Bot thoillis me to de in panis smart.   18
    O Venus quene! thow causs hir mynd rewart: O Venus!
    For be þe graue, first lufe in to me grew;   make her
    Sen I mon [de, adew, luvaris, adew].   21 relent.

    Now lat me lady do quhat evir scho will,   22
    Baith trest & trew my hairt sall nevir fel;
    Small honor is, hir scherwand for to spill,
    Sen þat my deth to hir may nocht awail;   25
    Ane blenk of hir but dout wald mak me haill: A blink from
    My hairt is gon, my face is paill of hew;   her would
    Sen I [mon de, adew, luvaris, adew].   28 make me
      whole.

    Addew, addew, my dule and my delyte,   29
    Adew, fairweill, my freind & eik my fo,
    Adew, my pane & plesans most perfyte,
    Addew, addew, my weill & eik my wo,   32
    Fairweill, for now for euirmoir I go,
    Fairweill, I will my sepultur persew;
    Sen I mon de, addew, luvaris, adew.   35

16.

[Departe, departe, departe.]

Quod Scott off þe Maister of Erskyn.

[leaf 245 b, p. 546]
Alas! I must leave my love.

Departe, departe, departe,
Allace! I most departe
Frome hir þat hes my hart,
   With hairt full soir,   4
Aganis my will indeid,
And can find no remeid,
I wait the panis of deid
   Can do no moir.   8

Happy I'll never be till I see her again.

Now most I go, allace!   9
Frome sicht of hir sueit face,
The grund of all my grace,
   And souerane: 12
Quhat chanss that may fall me
Sall I nevir mirry be,
Vnto þe tyme I se
   My sweit agane.   16

Departe, departe, departe.

I go, and wait no*ch*t quhair,   17
I wandir heir and thair,
I weip and sichis rycht sair,
        W*ith* panis smart;
Now most I pass away away   21
In wildirness & wilsu*m* way;
Allace! this wofull day
        We suld depa*r*te.   24

My spreit dois quaik for dreid,   25
My thirlit hairt dois bleid,   My pierced
My panis dois exceid;   heart bleeds
                                            at the pros-
        Quhat suld I say?   28   pect of parting.
I wofull wycht allone,
Makand ane petouss mone,
Allace! my hairt is gone,
        For evir and ay.   32

Throw langour of my sueit,   33
So thirlit is my spreit,
My dayis ar most co*m*pleit,
        Throw hir absence: 36
Chryst, sen scho knew my smert,
Ingrawit in my hairt,
Becaus I most depa*r*te
        Frome hir presens.   40

Adew, my awin sueit thing,   41   [leaf 266, p. 547]
My joy and co*n*forting,   Adieu, my
My mirth and sollesing   own sweet love.
        Of erdly gloir: 44
Fair weill, my lady bricht,
And my reme*m*bra*n*ce rycht.
Fair weill, and haif gud nycht;
        I say no moir.   48

17.

[That evir I luvit allace þairfoir.]

[leaf 246, p. 547]
Alas, that ever I loved.

    That evir I luvit, allace þairfoir,
    This to be pynit with panis soir,
    Thirlit throw every vane and boir   3
        Without offenss
    Chryst send remeid, I say no moir
        Bot pacienss.   6

Grissal was not so patient as I.

    Grissal was nevir so pacient
    As I am for my lady gent,
    For in my mynd I so imprent   9
        Hir excellenss
    That of my deid I am content
        With pacienss.   12

How long shall I have to suffer?

    How lang sall I this lyfe inleid?
    That for hir saik do[1] suffer deid,
    But confort of hir gudly heid   15
        Or ȝit presens;
    I say no moir, christ send remeid
        With paciens.   18

I must betake me to patience, because I grow worse.

    On paciens I mon perforss,
    Sen þat I go frome weill to worss,
    Exorting chryst send hir remorss   21
        Of conscienss
    Sa crewaly hes keild my corss
        But pacienss.   24

Patience overcomes my grief.

    Paciens ourcumis all,
    And is ane vertew principall,
    Sen I am bund to leif in thrall   27
        With insolens,
    I mon sustene quhat so befall
        With pacienss.   30

---

[1] MS. reads "to."

But paciens I ȝow assure,
Nane may þe panis of lufe indure,
Nor ȝit in to that lufly bour 33
    Mak residens,
Without thay preif baith sueit and sour
    With paciens. 36

Without patience the pains of love cannot be endured.

Lufe is maid of sic ane kynd,
That be na forss it may be synd,
Bot only be of hummill mynd 39
    With parmanenss
To thoill, suppoiss þe hairt be pynd,
    With pacienss. 42

The passion of love is too powerful to be sundered from the soul.

18.

[Oppressit hairt, indure.]

Oppressit hairt, indure 1
In dolour and distress,
Wappit without recure
In wo remidiless ;
Sen scho is merciless, 5
And caussis all thy smert
Quhilk suld thy dolour dress ;
Indure oppressit hairt ! 8

*[leaf 246 b, p. 548]
Heart, be patient,
since she is merciless.*

Perforss tak paciens 9
And dre thy destany
To lufe but recompens
Is grit perplexitie ;
Of thyne aduersitie 13
Wyt thyself and no mo,
For quhen þat thow wes fre
Thow wald nocht hald þe so. 16

You should have kept your freedom.

You longed to test the power of love.	Thow la*n*git ay to prufe The strenth of luvis lair, And quhat kin thing wes lufe Quhilk now sett*is* the so sair.	17
It is useless to moan.	Off all thy wo and cair It mend*is* the no*ch*t to mene, Howbeid thow suld forfair, Thyself þe causs hes bene.	21 24
[leaf 247, p. 549] You freely chose her who slights thee now.	Quhe*n* thow wes weill at eiss And subiect to no wicht, Thow hir for lufe did cheiss Quhilk settis thy lufe at licht; And tho*ch*t thow knew hir slicht ȝit wald thow [nocht] refrane, Thairfoir it is bot rycht That thow indure þe pane.	25 29 32
My whole body is oppressed; why is this when I alwaysdetested thy wanton mind?	Bot ȝit my corpss allace, Is wra*n*gusly opprest Be the in to þis cace And bro*ch*t to grit wanrest, Quhy suld it so be drest, Be the, and daly pynd? Quhilk still it ay detest Thy wantoun folich mynd.	33 37 40
I always bade thee stay at home, but thou wouldst rake in the mire without grasping what thou didst most desire.	The blenkyne of ane E Ay gart the goif and glaik; My body bad lat be, And of thy siching slaik, Thow wald no*ch*t rest bot raik And lair the in þe myre, ȝit felȝeit thow to faik That thow did maist desyre.	41 45 48
	Tho*ch*t thow do murn and weip W*ith* inwart spreit opprest, Quhe*n* vþir me*n* tak*is* sleip Thow wantis the nychtis rest:	49

Scho quhome thow luvis best	53	
Off the takis littill tho*ch*t,		
Thy wo and grit wanrest		Thy love regards not
And cair scho countis no*ch*t.	56	thy woe.

Thairfoir go hens in haist	57	Therefore go hence,
My lango*u*r to lame*n*t.		and leave me at rest.
Do no*ch*t my body waist		
Quhilk nevir did co*n*sent,		
And tho*ch*t thow wald repent	61	
That thow hir hes pe*r*sewit,		
ȝit man thow stand co*n*tent		
And drynk þat thow hes brewit.	64	

19.

[𝔏eif lube & lat me leif allone.]

Leif luve and lat me leif allone	1	[leaf 247, p. 549]
At libertie, subiect to none;		Let me live without love.
For it may weill be sene vpone		
My bludless blaiknit ble;	4	
The tormenting, in tyme bygon,		
That skerss hes left bot skin and bon		
Throw fre*m*mitness of the.	7	

For thruch thy feid I fynd express	8	Cupid, thou art to blame
My only lady me*r*ciless		for my misery: my
Sa doggitless scho did me dress		lady is without mercy.
Wi*th* wo and misery;	11	She treated me unworthily.
Quhe*n* scho had welth and wantonness		
I had bot dollour and distress,		
Throw fre*m*mitness of the.	14	

To confort hir thow wes inclynd,	15	Thou wert inclined to
And hald my murny*ng* in my mynd,		comfort her, but to keep
I fand hir of ane staffage kynd		me mourning.
Bath staitly, strange, and he.	18	

	Scho wes vncurtass & vnkynd,	
	It wes hir play to se me pynd,	
	Throw [fremmitness of the].	21

[leaf 247 b, p. 550]
Thou lettest my love sleep softly

  Thow held hir curage he on loft,   22
  And ted my tendir hairt lyk toft,
  I knaw how costly I wes coft
    Quhen scho ȝeid frank and fre :   25
  Thow sufferit hir to sleip full soft,

whilst thou left me mirthless.

  Quhair mirthles I wes marterit oft,
    Throw fremitness of the.   28

Thou knowest I burned to live under thy law,

  Cupeid thow kennis I burd to knaw,   29
  The langsum leving in thy law;
  Bot this is nocht þe first ourthraw
    That thow hes done to me.   32

now I fear thee not. Reason rules,

  Bot of the now I stand nocht aw,
  Sen ressoun dois my benner blaw
    Aganis the feid of the.   35

  This lady is so gud ane gyd,   36
  Scho lattis me nevir gang on syd,
  Bot teichis me both tyme & tyd
    Retent befoir myne E,   39

and she never lets me err.

  Quhome in to lippin and confyd;
  I slip, and lattis all ourslyd;
    Aganis the feid of the.   42

20.

[𝕿𝖍𝖔𝖈𝖍𝖙 𝕴 𝖎𝖓 𝖌𝖗𝖎𝖙 𝖉𝖎𝖘𝖙𝖗𝖊𝖘𝖘.]

[leaf 247 b, p. 550]

  Thocht I in grit distress
  Suld de in to dispair,
  I can get no redress
  Of ȝow my lady fair,   4

Thocht I in grit distress.

Howbeid my tyme I wair
Alhaill in ȝour scherwyce,   *You heed not my service.*
Ȝe compt nocht of my cair,
    I fynd ȝow ay so nyce.   8

It dois ȝow ay delyt   9   *You delight in chiding me.*
To wit me in distress.
Sic is ȝour haill dispyt
And grit vnfathfulness;   12
The mair I do me dress   *The more I try to serve*
To be at ȝour devyce,
My guerdoun is the less   *the less is my guerdon.*
    I find ȝow ay so nyss.   16

Ay tresting for to speid   17   *Always hoping to succeed, I've upset my heart.*
I haif my hairt ourset,
Quhair þat I fynd bot feid
My langour for to lett;   20
I seik the watter hett
In vndir the cauld yce,
Quhair na regaird I gett
    I fynd ȝow ay so nyss.   24

Belevand ay for grace   25
I hald my hairt on loft,
Bot now I say, allace   *I am sorry I ever sought your love.*
That evir I it socht!   28
I fynd ȝour fenȝeit thocht
Vncertane as þe dyce,
Thairfoir I compt it nocht
    I fynd ȝow ay so nyce.   32

Lang tyme ȝe haif me pruffit   33
And evir fund me trew,
Bot now that I haif luvit
Rycht sair I may it rew.   36
First quhen I did persew,   *When first I followed I weened that you were wise. Farewell!*
I wont ȝe had bene wyss,
Bot now fairweill, adew!
    I find ȝow ay so nyss.   40

21.

[𝔏angour to leibe, allace.]

[leaf 251, p. 557]
My labour is vain;

Langour to leive, allace!
My labour is in vane,
Sen þair is nowþir grace,
Nor ȝit rewaird agane.   4

I am without her love,

Quhat sall I do [o]r say,
I am with sorrow slane,
And dyis nicht & day
Withowt hir luve agane.   8

though faithful

Was nevir man in erd,
Moir faithfull & moir plane,
Suppois it be my werd
To luve vnluvit agane.   12

through many years.

I do luve best allane
My lady souerane,
Thir ȝeiris mony ane,
Withowt hir luve agane.   16

She let me woo,

For nowdir wald schew rew
Nor beir me at disdane,
Bot lute me ay persew
Withowt hir luve agane.   20

and kept me with feigned words

Hir fenȝeit wordis fals,
Of richt not maid me fane,
And held me in the hals,
To lufe vnluvit agane.   24

and bright glances.

And als the luik vnleill
Of hir bricht fair ene twane,
Gart me beleif alhail
To haif hir luve agane.   28

Now that I see her character,

I shall turn my heart from her,

Bot sen I se hir hairt
And mynd is vncertane,
I sall in tyme rewairt
My luve frome hir agane.   32

Sen scho hes nowþir rewth
Nor mercy, suth to sane, *and let false-*
Lat falset to vntrewth, *hood join with deceit,*
And trest to trew agane.   36 *and honesty with truth.*

And sen my hairt is fre, *[leaf 251 b, p. 558]*
I bid not for to lane,
I sall awysit be *I do not con-*
Or I hir luve agane.   40 *ceal that I*

Thairfoir, my hairt tak heid *shall be care-*
Quhome for thow suffer pane, *ful before I love again:*
And luik weill for remeid,
Or þat thow luve agane.   44

Scho þat the list to luve *see that thou*
Se thow with hir remane, *remain true to her who*
And nevir moir remvue, *loves you.*
Bot luve hir best agane.   48

22.
[Favour is fair in luvis lair.]
[leaf 251 b, p. 558]

Favour is fair / in luvis lair, *Love goes by favour;*
ȝit freindschip mair / bene to commend; *friendship is more praise-*
Bot quhair despair / bene adwersare, *worthy. Where the*
Nothing is thair / bot wofull end.   4 *enemy is despair, there is no hope.*

Off men I mene / in scherwice bene, *I bemoan*
Of Venus quene / but conforting; *those in the service of*
Be thame I wene / that mon sustene, *Venus, who are unsuc-*
The kairis kene / of Cupeid king.   8 *cessful.*

Continwance / in Cupeidis dance, *It was my*
But discrepance / withowt remeid, *lot to join in Cupid's dance*
Sic was my chance / in observance, *without re-*
But recompance / my lyfe to leid.   12 *ward.*

Hir court he[s] jo / quhair evir thay go, *The courtiers*
The lyfe is so / scho dois thame len, *of Venus have joy: but the*
Quhair his hes wo / withowttin ho, *victims of Cupid have*
He is sic fo / till faythfull men.   16 *woe without halt.*

I speak from experience. Cupid's dart may yet make her repent of her treatment of me.

I speik expart / suppois I smart
That scho hes gart / me thus lament,
Bot this same darte / may causs hir harte,
Heir eftirwart / also repent. 20

[leaf 252, p. 559]

Happy is the man free from love's pains.

Sen so I se / to leif in le,
At libbertie / is weill but wo,
Happie is he / I say for me,
Quhen he is fre / can hald him so. 24

23.

[Returne thee, hairt, hamewart agane.]

Quod Alexander Scott to his hert.

[leaf 252 b, p. 560]

Return!

Returne the, hairt, hamewart agane, 1
And byd quhair thow was wont to be;

thou art a fool, O my heart, to suffer on account of one who loves thee not.

Thow art ane fule to suffer pane,
For luve of hir, þat luvis not the. 4
My hairt, lat be sic fantesie;
Luve nane bot as thay mak the causs,
And lat hir seik ane hairt for the;
For feind a crum of the scho fawis. 8

Why shouldst thou be thrall?

To quhat effect sowld thow be thrall 9
But thank, sen thow hes thy fre will,
My hairt be nocht sa bestiall,
Bot knaw quho dois the guid or ill; 12
Remane with me, and tary still,
And se quha playis best their pawis,
And lat fillok ga fling hir fill;
For feind a ccrum of the scho fawis. 16

Thocht scho be fair, I will not fenȝie, 17
Scho is the kynd of vþiris ma;

[leaf 253, p. 261]

She is not the only woman:

For quhy thair is a fellone menȝie,
That semis gud, and ar not sa. 20
My hairt tak nowdir pane nor wa,
For Meg, for Meriory, or ȝit Mawis,
Bot be thow glaid, and latt hir ga;
For feind a ccrum of the scho fawis. 24

Becaus I find scho tuik in ill, 25
At hir departing thow mak na cair;   *let her go.*
Bot all begyld, go quhair scho will,
Beschrew the hairt that mane maikis mair. 28
My hert be mirry lait and air,
This is the fynall end and clauss;
And latt hir fallow ane filly fair,
For feind a crum of the scho fawis. 32

24.

[In June the jem of joy and geme.]

In June the jem / of joy, and geme 1   [leaf 255 *b*, p. 566]
This present to compyle express,   This June I am happy,
But hurt, but wem / or wind to stem,
Inarmit I am / with haviness. 4
    Wantone in weill but wo,
    Glaid without greif also,
    And fre of every fo   and free from every foe.
        That I confess. 8

I maik it plane / for luve agane 9   I shall not be love-sick again.
Thair sall no sorrow in me synk;
Nor ȝit in vane / to suffer pane
To stop frome sleip, frome meit or drink, 12
    Thair is no lady fre
    That and scho favour me,
    Scho will nocht thoill to se
        Me pyne I think. 16

Be scho content / of corss & rent 17   If she be willing,
All sal be hirss that I may get hir,
Will scho absent / hyne sall I went,
And at als littill valor set hir. 20
    Quhair power ma not plaiss,
    Adew without diseiss,   I am ready;
    Als gud luve cumis as gais
        Or raþir bettir. 24

Thair is nocht ane winche þat I se.

<small>but I will put up with no airs.</small>

Quhen scho growis heich / I draw on dreich   25
To vesy and behald the end,
Quhen scho growis skeich / I byd on beich,
To lat hir in the brydill bend.   28
    Quhen schow growis meik and tame,
    Scho sal be wylcome hame,
    Gif scho my luve quytclame
        I sall nocht kend.   32

Pleiss scho to rew / I sall persew   33
With subiect scherwyice every sessone,
Be scho vntrew / fair weill, adew,
For as scho chaingis I sall cheiss one.   36

<small>If she be faithful, I'll be true.</small>

    Bot gif scho steidfast stand,
    And be nocht wariand,
    I am at hir command
        Conforme to ressone.   40

25.

[𝔗hair is nocht ane winche þat 𝔍 se.[1]]

<small>[leaf 256, p. 567]</small>

Thair is nocht ane winche þat I se   1
Sall win ane wantage of me;
Be scho fals, I sal be sle,

<small>No false maid shall win my love.</small>

    And say to dispyt hir;   4
Be scho trew, I will confyd,
Will scho remane, I sall abyd;
Will scho slip, I will bot slyd,
    And so sall I quyt hir.   8

Be scho constant and trew,   9
I sall evir hir persew;
Be scho fals, than adew
    No langer I tary.   12
Be scho fathfull in mynd,
I sal be to hir inclynd;
Be scho strange and vnkynd,
    I gif hir to fary.   16

---

[1] Ascribed to A. Scott: no author is given by Bannatyne.

Be scho haltand and he	
Rycht swa sall scho fynd me;	17 *To a proud girl I shall be proud.*
Be scho lawly and fre,	
The suth I sall say hir.	20
Be scho secreit and wyiss,	
I sall await on hir scherwyiss	
Will scho glaik and go nyiss,	
I leif hir to play hir.	24

And I magyn my mailis,	25
I sall feid hir with taillis,	
Thocht my sallis haif no seillis,	
I sall leir hir to fan.	28
Be scho wylie as ane tod,	*A cunning one shall not cheat me.*
Quhen scho winkis I sall nod;	
Scho sall nocht begyle me, be god,	
For ocht that scho can.	32

26.

Quod Scott quhen his wyfe left him.[1]

[leaf 256, p. 567]

To luve vnluvit it is ane pane,	
For scho þat is my souerane,	
Sum wantoun man so he hes set hir,	3 *A wanton has taken my love.*
That I can get no lufe agane,	
Bot brekis my hairt, & nocht the bettir.	5

Quhen þat I went with þat sweit may,	
To dance, to sing, to sport and pley,	
And oft tymes in my armis plet hir;	8
I do now mvrne both nycht & day,	*I mourn her loss,.*
And brekis my hairt, & nocht the bettir.	10

Quhair I wes wont to se hir go,	[leaf 256 b, p. 568]
Rycht trymly passand to and fro,	
With cumly smylis quhen þat I met hir;	13
And now I leif in pane & wo	*and live in pain,.*
And brekis [my hairt, & nocht the bettir].	15

[1] This note is appended to the poem in the MS.

But I am a fool to kill myself with melancholy,

Quhattane ane glaikit fule am I,
To slay my self with malancholy,
Sen weill I ken I may nocht get hir, 18
Or quhat suld be the caus, and quhy,
To brek [my hairt, and nocht the bettir]. 20

as good love comes as goes. I'll choose another.

My hairt, sen thow may nocht hir pleiss,
Adew, as gude lufe cumis as gaiss,
Go chuss ane vdir, and forʒet hir; 23
God gif him dolour and diseiss,
That brekis thair hairt, and nocht the bettir. 25

27.
[Quha lykis to luve.]

[leaf 285 b, p. 626]
He who would love will have to suffer.

Quha lykis to luve / or þat law pruve, 1
Lat him beleif this lyfe to leid;
His mynd sall moif / but rest or ruve,
With diuerss doulouris to þe deid: 4
 He sall tyne appetyte
 And meit and sleip gife quyte,
 And want þe way perfyte
  To find remeid. 8

He sall nocht wit / quhiddir þat it 9
Be panefull, plesand, weill, or wo;
To stand, or sit / remoif or flit,
To gang, to ly, to byd, or go: 12
 No wit sal be degest
 To heir, se, smell, nor test;
 Bot as a brutall best
  He sall be so. 16

[leaf 286, p. 627]
and when once smitten he cannot shake off his bonds.

Fle thocht he wald / lufe sall him hald, 17
Within þe dungeoun of dispair;
Quhyle hett, quhyle cald / a thowsandfald,
His purpoiss sal be heir and thair; 20
 He sall hald wisdome vyce,
 And vertew of no pryce,
 Bot as a fule vnwyce
  So sall he fair. 24

This is the quhy / and causs þat I 25 *That's why I complain.*
Compleue so peteously in plane,
I lufe þe wy / will nocht apply,
Nor grant to gife / me grace agane : 28
    The moir scheruice I do
    The moir fremmit is scho,
    Without respect vnto
             My crewall pane. 32

ȝe luvaris se / gife þat this be 33 *From my experience learn why all good men condemn*
Ane lyfe þat all gude men malignis ;
I say for me / it is to fle
Aboif þe pest and plaig þat ringis : 36
    Quhilk is bot curius,
    Ay woid and furius,
    Ane[1] fyre sulfurius   [1] MS. And
             That men doun bringis. 40

My breþir deir / we most forbeir, 41
And fra this sinfull lyfe evaid ws ;   *this sinful life ;*
Lat ressoun steir / ȝour hairtis inteir,
And nocht thoill lathly lust to leid ws ; 44
    Quhilk is þe verry net   *it is a device of the devil.*
    That satane for ws set,
    To causs ws quyt forȝet
             The Lord þat maid ws. 48

28.

[Lo! quhat it is to luve.]

Lo! quhat it is to lufe, 1 *[leaf 286, p. 627]*
  Lerne ȝe that list to prufe,
Be me, I say, / that no ways may   *Love is*
  The grund of greif remvfe ; 4
Bot still decay, / both nycht and day :
  Lo quhat it is to lufe. 6

  Lufe is ane fervent fyre, 7 *a fire.*
  Kendillit without desyre ;

	Schort plesour, lang displesour,	
[leaf 286, p. 627]	Repentence is the hyre;	10
	Ane pure tressour, / without mesour;	
	Lufe is ane fervent fyre.	12

	To lufe and to be wyiss,	13
	To rege with gud adwyiss;	
	Now thus, now than, / so gois the game,	
	Incertane as[1] the dyiss: [1] MS. reads 'is.'	16
It drives away wisdom.	Thair is no man, / I say, that can,	
	Both lufe and to be wyiss.	18

Flee from its snares.	Fle alwayis frome þe snair,	19
	Lerne at me to be ware;	
	It is ane pane / and dowbill trane	
	Of endles wo and cair:	22
	For to refrane / that denger plane,	
	Fle alwayis frome þe snair.	24

29.

[Quhome sould I wyt of my mischance.]

[leaf 287, p. 629]	Quhome sould I wyt of my mischance,	1
Cupid! who should I chide but thee?	Bot Cupeid king of variance?	
	Thy court, without considerance,	
	Quhen I it knew,	4
	Or evir made þe observance,	
	Sa far I rew.	6

	Thow and thy law ar instrumentis	7
	Off diuerss inconvenientis;	
	Thy scheruice mony soir repentis,	
	Knawing þe quarrell;	10
	Quhen body, honor, & substance schentis	
	And saule in perrell.	12

What is thy homage but grief and pain.	Quhat is thy manrent bot mischeif,	13
	Sturt, angir, grunching, yre, and greif,	
	Evill lyfe, and langour but releif,	
	Off woundis wan;	16

Displesour, pane, and he repreif	
Off god and man!	18

Thow loviss thame þat lowdest leis,	19	Thou lovest the loudest liars.
And followis fastest on þame [that] fleis;		
Thow lychtleis all trew properteis		
Off lufe express,	22	
And markis quhair nevir styme thow seis,		
Bot hittis be gais[s].	24	

Blynd buk, bot at þe bound thow schutis,	25	Thou only shootest at those who are bound.
And þame forbeiris þat the rebutis;		
Thow ryvis þair hartis ay fra þe rutis,		Thou tearest out the hearts
Quhilk ar thy awin,	28	of those who are thine own.
And cureis þame, curis nocht thre cutis		
To be misknawin.	30	

Thow art in freyndschip with þi fo,	31	Thou art friendly with thine enemies, and at enmity with thy friends.
And fremmit to thy freynd also,		
Thow flemis all faythfull men the fro		
Of steidfast thocht,	34	
Regarding non bot þame ago,		
That curis the nocht.	36	

Thow chirreiss þame þat with þe chyddis,	37	
And baneiss þame with þe abydis:		
Thow hess þi horne ay in þair sydis,		Those who trust thee prosper least.
That cannocht fle;	40	
Thay furdir werst in the confydis,		
I say for me.	42	

30.

It cumis ȝow luvaris to be laill.

It cumis ȝow luvaris to be laill		[leaf 236 b, p. 528]
Off body, hairt, & mynd alhaill,		Faithfulness is becoming
And thocht ȝe with ȝour ladyis daill	3	in lovers.
Ressoun,		
Bot and ȝour faith and lawty faill		
Tressoun.		

You may sue if you are constant.	ȝe may with honesty persew,
	 Gif ȝe be constant, trest, & trew;
	 Thocht than vnrycht thay on ȝow rew 9
	                Ressoun,
	 Bot be ȝe fund dowbill, adew
	                Tressoun.

Give them your service.	ȝour hummill scheruice first resing thame,
	 For that to ȝour intent sall bring thame;
	 With leif of ladeis thocht ȝe thing thame 15
	                Ressoun
	 Bot eftirwart and ȝe maling thame
	                Tressoun.

Never incommode them.	Do nevir the deid that ma diseiss thame,
	 Bot wirk with all ȝour mind to meiss thame;
	 To tak ȝour plesour quhen it pleiss thame 21
	                Resoun,
	 Bot with vntrewth and ȝe betraiss thame
	                Tressoun.

Defend their reputation. [leaf 237, p. 529]	Defend thair fame quha evir fyle thame,
	 And ay with honest havingis style thame;
	 To Venus, als suppois ȝe wyle thame 27
	                Ressoun,
	 Bot be ȝe frawdfull and begyle thame
	                Tressoun.

Recollect that a little service will not content them.	ȝe suld considdir or ȝe taik thame,
	 That littill scheruice will nocht staik thame;
	 Get ȝe ane goldin hour to glak thame 33
	                Ressoun,
	 Bot be ȝe frawdfull & forsaik thame
	                Tressoun.

Be discreet	Be secreit, trew, and plane allwey;
	 Defend þair fame baith nycht and day;
	 In prevy place suppoiss ȝe play 39
	                Ressoun,
	 Bot be ȝe ane clattrer, harmisay!
	                Tressoun.

Be courtas in ʒour cumpany,
For that sall causs thame to apply;
Thocht þat thay lat ʒow with thame ly 45
                Ressoun,   *and courteous,*
Bot be ʒe fund vnfaithfull, fy !
                Tressoun.

Wey weill thir versis that I wryt ʒow;
Do ʒour devoir[1] quhen þat thay lat ʒow;   *and do your duty when*
To lufe ʒour ladies quho can wyt ʒow? 51 *they permit you.*
                Ressoun
Do ʒe the contrair, heir I quyt ʒow
                Tressoun.

31.

[Fra raige of ʒowth the rynk hes rune.]

Fra raige of ʒowth the rynk hes rune,   1 [leaf 280, p. 615]
And ressone tane the man to tune,   *When the storm of*
The brukle body than is wvne   *youth is over, and reason*
   And maid ane veschell new,   4 *enters the mind, then*
For than thruch grace he is begune   *is the body as if made*
The well of wisdome for to kune;   *anew.*
Than is his weid of vertue spune
   Trest weill this taill is trew.   8

For ʒowth and will ar so consorss   9
Withowt þat wisdome mak devorss,   *Youth runs wild*
Thay rin lyk wyld vndantit horss
   But brydillis, to and fro.   12
Thair curage sa ourcumis thair corss,
Thrwcht heit of blude it hes sic forss
Bot gif the mynd haif sum remorss
   Of God, all is ago.   16

This wid fantastyk lust but lufe,   17
Dois so ʒung men to madness mvfe,
That thay ma nowþir rest nor rufe,
   Till thay mischeif þair sellis.   20

    [1] MS. reads 'devior.'

Fra raige of ȝowth the rynk hes rune. [31.

with women.

Haif thay thair harlottis in behufe,
Thay sussy nocht thair god abufe;
Thair fame, thair wirschep, nor reprufe
    Off honour nor ocht ellis.   24

Love should be mixed with prudence, though some say that love controlled by sense is worthless.

Ferme luve with prudens suld be vsit,   25
Thocht sum allegeand to excus it,
Sayis¹ þat luve with witt inclusit
    Ȝit is nocht worth a buttoun.   28
Sic vane opinioun is confusit,
That man but ressoun may be rusit;
Quha bene with beistly lust abusit,
    I hald him bot ane muttoun.   32

Those who would be esteemed by women should be brave.

Quha wald in luve be estimat,   33
Suld haif þair hairtis ay elevat
With merciall myndis in doing þat,
    Mycht causs thair fais to dowt thame.   36
Thocht wemen self be temerat
Thay luve no man effeminat,
And haldis thame, bot I wat not quhat,
    That cannoch[t] be withowt thame.   40

[leaf 280 *b*, p. 616]

Ȝit man suld fauour thame, howbeid   41
Thay be bot necessar of neid;
Becauss we cum of thame, in deid,
    Thair personis suld be prysit.   44
As grund is ordand to beir seid,

Woman is born to bear children.

So is the woman born to breid
The fruct of man, and that to feid
    As nature hes dewysit.   48

Schort to conclude, I wald bath knew   49

Men should be loyal, and women honest.

That luvaris suld be leill and trew;
And ladeis suld all thingis eschew
    That ma thair honor smot.   52
Be permanent þat wald persew
And rin nocht reklesly to rew
Bot as I direct, Adew!
    Thuss I depairt, q[uod] Scott.   56

¹ MS. reads 'saying.'

Satires.

32.

The slicht remeid of luve.

Luvaris, lat be the frennessy of luve,	1	[leaf 122, p. 303]
And mvse nor mvrne no moir intill ȝour mind,		Lovers, mourn no more.
Bot sollace seik, and sorrow ay remove;		
Cast ȝow to conqueiss luve ane vþir kynd.		
For knew ȝe wemenis natur, course, & strynd,	5	Women are fickle:
Ȝe wald nocht be so trew to thair vntrewth		
Quhilkis hes no petie thocht ȝour hairtis be pynd,		they heed not your pain.
Nor of ȝour restless womenting no rewth.	8	
Bot wald ȝe rewill ȝow, keip this regiment:	9	If you'd rule,
Be subteill, secreit, sobir, in thair sicht,		
Facound of wordis, but feckill of intent,		keep your own counsel.
And nevir lat ȝour mowth and mynd go richt.		
Swey as thay swey, be blyth quhen thay ar licht,	13	Always agree with them:
And preiss ȝow ay in presenss to repair,		
Forvey no tyme, be reddy day and nicht		pretend to be at their call.
Vpoun ȝour kneis to serve thame soletare.	16	
Be prevy, pert, in presenss play with synis,	17	Never let them know what you think.
Be sicht or smyle lat non knaw ȝour intentis,		
Be verry war or that thay wit ȝour myndis;		
Be clenely cled in ȝour abilȝementis.		[leaf 122 b, p. 304]
Reuse nocht ȝour self, latt vþiris preiss ȝour rentis,	21	Dress well; do not boast; offer your services.
Bot offir thame ȝour daly observance		
Be tung; thocht naþir hairt nor mynd consentis		
Body and gudis to haif in govirnance.	24	

If refused, complain little; heed not the chatter, but press your suit another day.	Abuse bot breif, howbeid ȝe be said nay, And reckles nocht ȝour erand for the rane, Bot cast ȝow for to cum ane vþer day, And petously complene ȝour woles pane, Saying ȝe ar both secreit, trew, and plane; With this, part wreth and fremmit to, but faid	25 29
Leave them to relent.	For cum the freindschip of thair syd agane : I mak ȝow seur ȝe sall nocht miss remeid.	32
Keep friends with those who can help you; promise them gifts, though you never give any; speak fair till you get what you want.	Hald thame in hand, quhilkis may ȝow help at neid, And hecht thame giftis howbeid ȝe gif thame nocht, For thair gud word sall rathest cause ȝow speid, And thrwch their creddence to ȝour purpoiss brocht. Speik fair, till ȝe haif gottin that ȝe socht; Be wyiss and war, and watt thame ay with wylis; For be the wy that all the warld wrocht, Maist witt hes hie, that moniest oursylis.	 37 40
Solicit a secret meeting. Make your moan when it will avail; flatter them,	Meikly solist to meit in secreit place, Syne mak ȝour mane quhan it may maist avelȝie, Be richt demvre & graif quhen ȝe ask grace, Bot be ȝe rank quhen thay begin to relȝie. Fleiche with fyisene ffor feir sumpart ȝe felȝie :	41 45
and without difficulty you can win.	And swa but pane ȝe may lufe parramowris; Be softe of speiche, bot spair nocht till asselȝie, Wyn anis the entress, & the houss is ȝowris.	 48
Be discreet, and protect the lady's reputation.	Bot ȝit ȝe may mishaif ȝow in sum caice, And ȝe defend nocht damissellis defame, For practik is to play, syne hald ȝour peice, And counsale keip, ffor hurting of thair name. Richswa forbeir a manis wyfe for blame, And hald ȝow koy in quiet quhill ȝe get her; As for a weddow wirk weill on hir wame, I knaw no craft sall cause hir lufe ȝow bettir.	49 53 56

33.

Ane ballat maid to þe derisioun and scorne of wantoun wemen.

[leaf 128 b, p. 316]

Ʒe lusty ladyis luke
The rakles lyfe ʒe leid,
Hant nocht in hoile or nuke
To hurt ʒour womanheid;
I reid, for best remeid,   5
Forbeir all place prophane:
Gife this be caus of feid,
I sall not said agane.   8

Ladies, beware of leading thoughtless lives. Hurt not your womanhood.

Quhat is sic luve bot lust,   9
A lytill for delyte,
To hant that game robust,
And beistly appetyte;
I nowdir fleische nor flyte,   13
To tell the trewith certane;
Taik ʒe this in despyte,
I sall not said agane.   16

Such love is but lust.

The wysest scho may sone   17
Sedusit be and schent;
Syne fra the deid be done,
Perchance sall soir repent;
Ouir lait is till lament   21
Fra belly dow not lane,
To try in tyme take tent:
I sall not said agane.   24

The wisest maid may be seduced, and repentance will not hide her shame.

Lycht wynchis luve will fawin,   25
Evin lyk ane spanʒeollis lawchter
To lat hir wamb be clawin
Be thame list geir betawcht hir;
For conʒie ʒe may chawcht hir,   29
To sched hir schankis in twane,
And nevir speir quhais awcht hir:
I sall not said agane.   32

Light wenches feign love like a brood of spaniels, and can be had for money.

[leaf 129, p. 317]	Thocht bruckill wemen hantis In lust to leid thair lyvis, And wedow men þat wantis To steill a pair of swyvis;	33
Households never thrive where the wives are unfaithful.	Bot quhair that mareit wyvis Gois by thair husbandis bane, That houshald nevir thryvis; I sall not said agane.	37 40
Maids should not let men take liberties,	It settis not madynis als To latt men lowis thair laice Nor clym about menis halss, To clap, to kiss, nor braice,	41
nor should they have secret meetings.	Nor round in secreit place; Sic treitment is a trane To cleive thair quaver-caice: I sall not said agane.	45 48
Farewell to their chastity when wenches begin to fondle.	Fairweill with chestetie, Fra wenchis fall to chucking, Thair followis thingis thre To gar thame ga in gucking, Brasing, Graping, and Plucking; Thir foure the suth to sane, Enforsis thame to fucking: I sall not said agane.	49 53 56
Some girls like dancing,	Sum luvis new cum to toun, With jeigis to mak thame joly, Sum luvis dance vp and doun, To meiss thair malancoly;	57
others like men.	Sum luvis lang trollie-lolly, And sum of frigging fane, Lyk fillokkis full of folly: I sall not said agane.	61 64
Some moonsick maids are got with child,	Sum monebrunt madynis myld, At nonetyd of the nicht, Ar chappit vp with chyld, But coile or candill-licht;	65

33.] *Ane ballat maid to þe scorne of Wantoun Wemen.*

 Sua sum said maidis hes slicht   69 [leaf 129 *b*, p. 318]
 To play, and tak no pane,
 Syne chift thair seid fra sicht: and some procure
 I sall not said agane.   72 abortions.

 Sum thinkis na schame to clap   73 Some girls are not
 And kiss in opin wyiss;   ashamed to kiss openly,
 Sum can-nocht keip hir gap
 Fra lansing as scho lyiss;
 Sum gois so gymp in gyiss,   77 others would rather be
 Or scho war kissit plane,   thrice debauched than
 Scho['d] leir be japit thryiss: be caught doing so.
 I sall not [said againe].   80

 Moir gentrice is to jott   81 Those in silk attire are
 Vndir ane silkin goun,   readiest for the game of
 Nor ane quhyt pittecott   love.
 And reddyar ay boun;
 The denkest / sonnest doun,   85
 The farest / But refrane,
 The gayest / Grittest loun:
 I sall not said again.   88

 The moir degest and grave,   89 Grave, fastidious,
 The grydiar to grip it;   pale-faced girls are the
 The nycest to ressave,   most eager.
 Vpoun the nynnis will nip it;
 The quhytliest will quhip it,   93
 And nocht hir hurdeis hane;
 The less the lerger hippit:
 I sall not said agane.   96

 Loe! ladeis gif this bie,   97 Ladies, I give you good
 Ane gud counsale I geif ȝow,   counsel:
 To saive ȝour honestie,
 Fra sklander to releif ȝow;
 Bot ballatis ma to breif ȝow,   101 but if you do not take it,
 I will nocht brek my brane,   I shall not distress myself.
 Suppois ȝe sowld mischeif ȝow;'
 I sall not said agane.   104

34.

[I mvse and mervillis in my mind.]

<small>[leaf 254, p. 563]
How shall I describe women's ways?</small>

I mvse and mervellis in my mind,
Quhat way to wryt, or put in verss,
The quent consaitis of wemen-kynd,   3
Or half thair havingis to reherss :
   I fynd thair haill affectioun
   So contrair thair complexioun.   6

<small>Though they tolerate no disloyal man, yet they are deceitful.</small>

For quhy no leid vnleill they leit,
Vntrewth expresly thay expell ;
ȝit thay ar planeist and repleit,   9
Of falset and dissait thair sell :
   So find I thair affectioun
   Contrair thair complexioun.   12

<small>Contemning fools, yet few of them are wise ; despising the greedy, they are covetous.</small>

Thay favour no wayis fuliche men,
And verry few of thame ar wyiss,
All gredy personis thay misken,   15
And thay ar full of covettyiss :
   So find [I thair affectioun]
   Contrair [thair awin complexioun].   18

<small>Pretending to keep secrets, they reveal them.</small>

I can thame call bot kittie vnsellis,
That takkis sic maneris at thair motheris,
To bid men keip thair secreit counsailis,   21
Syne schaw the same agane till vþiris :
   So find I thair affectioun
   Contrair thair awin complexioun.   24

<small>They laugh with those they hate, and lament when with their friends.</small>

Thay lawch with thame that they dispyt,
And with thair lykingis thay lament ;
Of thair wanhap thay ley the wyt   27
On thair leill luvaris innocent :
   So fynd [I thair affectioun]
   Contrair [thair awin complexioun].   30

Thay wald be rewit, and hes no rewth,
Thay wald be menit, and no man menis,
Thay wald be trowit, and hes no trewth, 33
Thay wiss thair will, that skant weill wenys :
   So fynd [I thair affectioun]
   Contrair [thair awin complexioun]. 36

They seek for pity, though they have none for others.

Thay forge the freindschip of the fremmit,
And fleis the favour of ther freind*is* ;
Thay wald with nobill men be nemmit, 39
Syne laittandly to lawar leindis :
   So find I thair affectioun
   Contrair thair complexioun. 42

They make friends of [leaf 254 b, p. 564] *strangers, and flee from their friends; they wish to be named as the acquaintances of nobles, while in secret they incline to the base born.*

Thay lichtly sone, and covettis quickly ;
They blame ilk body, and thay blekit,
Thay eindill fast, and dois ill lickly ; 45
Thay sklander saikles, & thay suspectit :
   So find [I thair affectioun]
   Contrair [thair awin complexioun]. 48

They disparage what they covet: blame, become jealous, and slander without reason, while their own characters are open to doubt.

Thay wald haif all men bund & thrall
To thame, and thay for to be fre ;
Thay covet ilk man at thair call, 51
And thay to leif at libirtie :
   So fynd [I thair affectioun]
   Contrar [thair awin complexioun]. 54

They want men to be their slaves, but wish to be free.

Thay tak delyt in merciall deidis,
And ar of nature tremebund ;
Thay wald men nvreist all their neid*is*, 57
Syne confortles lattis thame confound :
   So [find I thair affectioun]
   Contrar [thair awin complexioun]. 60

They delight in martial deeds, but are very timorous.

Thay wald haif wating on alway,
But gwerdoun, genȝeild, or rewaird,
Thay wald haif reddy scherwand*is* ay, 63
But recompans, thank, or rewaird :
   So find I thair affectioun
   Contrair [thair awin complexioun]. 66

They crave much service, but give no reward.

Ladies, be war þat plesand ar.

<small>The point of this writing is that women are the opposite of what they seem to be.</small>

The vertew of this writ and vigour,
Maid in comparisone it is,
That famenene ar of this figour,   69
Quhilk clippit is Antiphratis:
   For quhy thair haill affectioun
   Is contrair thair complexioun.   72

<small>Good women will not blame me for what I say.</small>

I wat, gud wemen will nocht wyt me,
Nor of this sedull be eschamit;
For be thay courtas, thay will quyt me;   75
And gif thay crab, heir I quytclame it:
   Confessand thair affectioun,
   Conforme to þair complexioun.   78

35.
[Ladies, be war þat plesand ar.]

<small>[leaf 276 b, p. 608]
Ladies, beware,</small>

Ladies, be war / þat plesand ar
   To menis appetyte,
That ȝe nocht rew / þat ȝe thame knew
   Throw þair lust and delyte.   4

<small>[leaf 277, p. 609]
men are false.</small>

For mony men / ar evill to ken
   þat luvis paramour,
With fenȝeit mynd, fals and vnkynd
   Bringis ȝow to dishonour.   8

<small>They'll leave you to beguile others:</small>

Quhen thay haif ane / with flattry tane,
   Begylit with a trane,
Then with ane vddir / thay will confiddir
   And play þe contrar pane.   12

Thay will promit / giftis rycht grit,
   And sueir thay luve ȝow best;
Ȝow to begyle / with mony wyle
   Thair mynd takkis nevir rest.   16

<small>their hearts are subtle.</small>

Thair hairtis ar sett / with sittelness,
   For loif and nocht for lufe
Ȝow to dissaif / with dowbilness
   To ȝour schame and reprufe.   20

ʒe blindit luvaris luke.

O ladeis deir / I ʒow requeir,
Thair fals and fenʒeit fair,
Latt ay go henss / and tyne creddens
Beleving þame no mair.   24

Do not trust these false wooers.

36.

[Ʒe blindit lubaris luke.]

Bannatyne MS. **Maitland MS.**

Bannatyne MS.	Maitland MS.		
blindit luvaris luke	ʒe blindit luiffarris luke		[leaf 289, p. 633; Maitland MS. p. 262.]
ie rekless lyfe ʒe leid ;	The rekles lyfe ʒe leid ;		*Look, lovers, at your reckless lives.*
ipy the snair and huke	Espye þe snair and hwke		
iat haldis ʒow be þe heid :	4 Quilk hankis ʒow be þe heid :	4	
iairfoir, I reid remeid,	I hald it best remeid,		
) leife and lat it be ;	To leif and latt it be ;		
)r lufe hes non at feid	For luif hes none at feid		
)t fulis þat can nocht fle.	8 Bot fuilis þat can not flee.	8	
uhat is ʒour lufe bot lust,	Quhat is ʒour luif bot lust,		*Your love is lust;*
ne littill for delyte,	And litle for delyte,		
ne beistly game robust,	Ane beistlie game robust,		
) reif ʒour ressoun quyte ;	12 To reif ʒour rasoun quyte ;	12	*it steals your reason,*
ne fowsum appetyte,	Ane fulsum appetyte,		
iat strenth of persoun waikis ;	That strenth and persoun waikis ;		*and weakens your body.*
ne pastance vnperfyte,	Ane pastyme imperfyte,		
) smyte ʒow with þe glaikis.	16 To smote ʒow with þe glaikis.	16	
uhair sensuall lust proceidis,	Quhair¹ sensuall luste procedis,		*When lust comes to the front, it destroys honest love.*
ll honest lufe is pynd ;	All honest luif is pynd ;		
ma compair ʒour deidis,	I may compair ʒour deidis,		
nto ane brutall kynd ;	20 Vnto ane brutell kynd ;	20	
ra vertew be con[s]trynd	Quhair verteu is constrynd		
) follow vyce, considdir	To follow vyce, considder		
hat ressoun, wit, and mynd,	That rasoun, wit, and mynd,		
r all ago togiddir.	24 Ar all ago togidder.	24	
he wysest woman þairout,	The wyisast woman þair out,		*The wisest woman may be seduced without her realizing the shame.*
Tith wirdis may be wyllit	Withe wordis may be wylit		
o do þe deid but dout,	To do þat deid butt dout,		
hat honour hes exyllit :	28 Quilk honour hes exylit :	28	

¹ MS. reads "Qubair" *for* "Quhair."

	How mony ar begyllit,	How mony ar begylit,
	And few I fynd that chaipis;	And few we find þat chaipis;
You break your faith to detraud simple girls.	Thairfoir ȝour faithis ar fylit	Quhan soir ȝour faythe is fylit
	To frawd thay silly aipis.	32 To fraude thais sillie aipis. 32
You-lovers look for grace where there is none,	Ȝe mak regaird for grace	Ȝe mak regrat for grace
	Quhair nevir grace ȝit grew;	Quhan grace ȝit never grew;
	Ȝe lang to ryn the race	Ȝe lang to rin þat race
	That ane or baith sall rew;	36 That ane or boithe sall rew; 36
and really seek sorrow.	Ȝe preiss ay to persew	Ȝe prees ay to persew
	Thair syte and ȝour awin sorrow;	Thair sytt and ȝour awin sorrow;
	Ȝe trest to find thame trew,	Ȝe traist to find þame trew,
	That nevir wes beforrow.	40 That never was able forrow. 40
[leaf 289, p. 634] You men call in vain on Cupid and Venus.	Ȝe cry on Cupeid king,	Ȝe cry on Cupide king,
	And Venus quene in vane;	And on Venus quene in vane;
	Ȝe send all maner thing	Ȝe send all syndrie thing
	With trattillis thame to trane;	44 With trateis þame to trane; 44
	Ȝe preiche, ȝe fleich, ȝe frane;	Ȝe preche, to fleche þe stayne,
You groan until your sweethearts succumb.	Ȝe grane ay quhill thay grant;	Ȝe greue ay quhyll þai grant,
	Ȝour prectikis ar profane,	Ȝour practikis ar prophane,
	Pure ladeis to supplant.	48 Pure ladeis to supplant. 48
You shout as if you were being murdered.	Ȝe schowt as ȝe wer schent,	Ȝe schoute as ye war schent,
	Thay swoun to se ȝow smartit;	Thai swoun to see ȝou smartit;
	Ȝe rame as ȝe wer rent,	Ȝe rave as ȝe war rent,
Your lady loves are pitiful:	And thay ar rewthfull hairtit;	52 And thai ar reuthfull hartit; 52
	Ȝour play[s] ar sone peruertit,	Ȝour play is so pervertit
but when you get them with child you weary of them.	Fra þat thair belly ryss;	Quhyll ȝe gar thair bellie ryis;
	Thay wary ȝow þat gart it,	Than warye þai ȝow þat gart it,[1]
	And ȝe thame in lykwyss.	56 And ȝe þame in lykwyis. 56

[1] MS. reads "gartit."

There is lawful love,	Ȝit thair is lesum lufe	Ȝit þair is leifsum luif
	That lawchtfully suld lest;	That lauchfullie suld lest;
which merits no reproof;	He is nocht to reprufe	He is not to repruif
	That is with ane possest:	60 That is with on possest: 60
	That band I hald it best,	That band of luif is best
	And nocht to pass attour,	And not to pas attoure,
	Bot ȝe can tak no rest	Bot ȝe can not tak rest
	Quhill thay kast vp all four.	64 Quhyll þai cast vpe all foure. 64

ȝe blindit luvaris luke.

Sic luiffarris seindele mcittis,	but some men cannot see women without
Bot leill luif ay forloirn is;[7]	
67 Quhone þai bewaill and greittis,	
Sum of ȝow mokkis and skornis :	
ȝour hecht, your aythe mensworn is[8]	
ȝour lippis ar lyk byrd lyme ;	
I think ȝe want bot horniss,	
72 Off bukkis in belling tyme. 72	

ȝe trattil and ȝe tyist,	coaxing them to forget their reputations.
Quhyll þai forȝet þair fame ;	
ȝe trane þame to ane tryst,	
76 And þair ȝe get þame tane : 76	
Thai sassie not for schame,	
Nor comptis not quhat cum syne ;	
Bot quhone ȝe clair þair wame,	
80 Thai woltir oure lyk swyne. 80	

Thocht ȝoung perverst creaturis	[leaf 290, p. 635]
To þalȝardrie replaidis ;	
And aulde ageit rubiatouris,	
84 Thai will hant þe leittis of laidis ;	
Fra þai begin sic gaidis,	
To leif of þai ar laythe,	
Quhyll þat þai get thre blaidis,	
88 Off Venus boutting clayth. 88	

ȝe wantoun wowarris vagis	You wanton wooers would marry a harlot if she had money,
With þame þat hes þe cwnȝe ;	
And scho haue bismeir baggis	
92 ȝe grunche not at hir grunȝe : 92	
Rycht so ladyis will not sunȝe	
With waistit wowbattis rottin,	
Bot proudlie[9] þai will prwnȝe	
96 Quhair geir is to be gettin. 96	and women too look where there's property.

[1] The line originally read, "Thocht þat perwersit cratouris."
[2] The original reading was, "ȝit auld rubiatouris." The word "auld" seems to .ve "it" added in the MS. The editor of 1882 ed. reads "auldit."
[3] Substituted for "That." [4] Substituted for "quhill."
[5] Substituted for "Bot." [6] Substituted for "Rycht swa."
[7] MS. reads "forloirnis." [8] MS. reads "menswornis."
[9] Original reading "prcuielie."

This is not love,	Quhair money may ȝow moif,	Gif money may ȝou move,
	I hald it aweryce;	I hald it auarice;
	Thair is na constant lufe,	It is no constant luife,
	Bot commoun merchandyce:	Bot commoun merchandice: 100
	This ordour now is nyce,	That ordour new it is,
it is buying and selling.	Quhair lufe is sauld and coft,	Quhair luif is sauld and coft,
	It is ane dowhill vyce	It is ane double vyce
	To bring the Devill on loft. 104	To bring þe dewill aloft. 104

The bich the curtyk fannis;	The bitche þe curr doig faunis;
The wolf the wilrone vsis;	The wolffe þe wilroun vsis;
The mull frequentis þe annis,	The mwle frequentis þe anis,
And hir awin kynd abusis;	And hir awin kynd abusis; 108
Rycht swa þe meir refusis	Rycht so þe meir refusis
The¹ cursour for ane awer;	Ane cursoure for ane aver;
Swa few I fynd excusis,	Rycht few I find excusis,
Bot² women quhylss will wauer.	Bot women quhylis will wavir. 112

Ȝit poyettis ffew³ decreitis,	
Saif ane hecht⁴ Pasific.⁵	
Bot of ȝour sodomeitis	
In Rome and Lumbardie, 116	*Lines* 113 *to* 120 *not in*
In [N]aippillis⁶ [and] Italie,	*Maitland MS.*
I revolt against describing your conduct. To compt how ȝe converss,	
I vg for villanie	
Ȝour vycis⁷ to reherss. 120	

[leaf 290 b, p. 636]	Quhair lechery belappis	Quhair lichorie belappis
Lechery stops love.	All steidfast luve it stoppis; 122	All stedfast luife it stoppis;
	Quhair hurdome, ay vnhapp is⁸	For huredome ay onhapp is¹¹ 123
	With quenry, canis, and coppis.	With quenerie, cannis, and coppis.
	Ȝe prye⁹ ȝow at þair proppis,	Ȝe preif ȝow at þair proppis,
	Till hair and berd grow¹⁰ dapill;	Quhyll hair and berde bedapte,
	Ȝe cowet all kyn croppis,	Ȝe coveit all kynd of croppis,
	As Eua did the apill. 128	As eua did þe apte. 128

---

¹ Substituted for "ane." ² Substituted for "saif." ³ Substituted for "nane."
⁴ Added in another hand. ⁵ MS. indistinct; may be read *Percifie*.
⁶ After "aippillis" "and" is deleted in MS. ⁷ Substituted for "vsinges."
⁸ Written "vnhappis" in MS. ⁹ MS. may be read either prye or pryd.
¹⁰ Substituted for "be." ¹¹ Written "onhappis" in MS.

ȝe blindit luvaris luke.

us ȝe haif all the wyte,	This ȝe haue all þe wyte,	'Tis your fault
d thair mischeif ȝe mak it,	And þair mischeif ȝe mak it,	
at suld haif wit perfyte,	That suld haue witt perfyte,	
d wisdome[1] to abstrak it.	132 And rasoun to abstract it. 132	
ld ladeis than be lakkit,	Suld ladeis þan be lakit,	that there are so few good women.
ocht few of thame be gud?	Thocht few of þame be gude?	
r all dissait[2] thay tak it,	All þair dissait, þei tak it,	
ȝour awin flesch and blude.	136 Off ȝour awin flesche and blude.	

ald ȝe foirse þe forme,	137	If you understood the consequences
e fassoun, and þe fek,		
suld it fynd inorme,		you would see the enormity of bawdry.
ith bawdry ȝow to blek:	140 *Lines 137 to 144 not in*	
airfoir fle fra suspek,	*Maitland MS.*	
than, sa mot I thryfe,		
ir natouris ȝe neglek,		
d wantis ȝour wittis fyve.	144	

pardoun me of thiss	Appardone me of this	Pardon me if I have offended:
f ocht be to displeiss ȝow,	Gif ocht be to displeis ȝow,	
d quhair I mak a miss,	Gif I haue said amiss,	
y mynd sal be to meiss ȝow:	148 My mynd sal be to meiss ȝow. 148	
ir ressonis[3] ar to raiss ȝow		these reasons are to warn you.
a crymes[4] vndir coite,	*Lines 149 to 152 not in*	
[5] war ȝe say nocht: Wa iss[6] ȝow!	*Maitland MS.*	
od Allexander Scote.	152	

[1] Substituted for "ressoun."   [2] Substituted for "þair evill."
ubstituted for "rymes."   [4] Line read originally "Fra crymes and vndir coite."
[5] MS. read originally "Thairfoir," instead of "Or war."
[6] Written "waiss" in MS.

SCOTT.   F

Paraphrases of the Psalms.

37.

The first psalme.

Beatus vir.

[leaf 16, old paging; p. 91, new paging]

Happy is he who flees iniquity;

    Happie is hie / hes hald him fre
        Frome folkis of defame;
    Alwayis to fle / iniquite
        And sait of syn and schame.   4

    Bot hes his will / conforme vntill
        The Lordis command and law,
    Thame to fulfill / with purpoiss still
        Boith day and nicht to knaw.   8

he shall flourish like a tree by the river side.

    He sall haif brute / as tre on rute
        Endlang the rever plantit;
    To burge and schute / and sall gif frutt /
        In tyme as God hes grantit.   12

    Quhois leif and blaid / sall nevir faid /
        Bot fragrant ay be flureist;
    Quhois workis on braid / sall evir spraid
        And richtously be nvreist.   16

The wicked shall not sit in judgment.

    Sall non be so / off nochtis no
        Quhilk bene of cursit bind:
    Bot thay sall go / lyk dust and stro
        Bene vaneist with the wind.   20

    Evill men lykwyiss / sall nocht arryiss
        To judgement as the trust,
    Nor thame that lyiss / in syne of[t] syiss
        To counsale with the just.   24

    For air and lait / the lord weill wait
      The wayiss of vertewus men,
    And every gait / of wicket stait
        Sall perreiss owt of ken.   28

      Gloria Patri
    To fader gloir / be evirmoir,
      To sone and haly spreit;
    As wes afoir / now is in stoir,
      And ay sal be, so be it.   32

38.

The fyifty psalme.[1]

[leaf 16 b, p. 92]

Lord God deliuer me, allace!   O God, deliver me;
For thy grit mercy, rewth and grace,
Soir mornyng, grufling on my face,
          Rew on my miserie: 4
Als for the mvltitud and space
Off thy heich clemenss, heir my cace,
And my trespass expell and chace;
          Lord god deliuer me.   8

Wesche me, and mak my sawle serene   wash me from all iniquity.
Frome all iniquite that bene;
Clenge me of cryme and mak me clene,
          All vycis for to fle.   12
For my transgressioun haif I sene,   I have seen my transgression.
Quhilk tormentis me with tray and tene,
And ay my syn forgane myne ene;
          Lord god deliuer me.   16

Only to the I did offend,
May non my miss bot thow amend,   Thou alone canst amend me.
As by thy sermondis thow art kend,
          Ourcum all contrarie.   20

---

[1] Vulgate version, Fifty-first in English Bible.

>   In filth, lo I begyn and end,
>   By syn maternall I am send,
>   With vyce I vaneiss and mon wend;
>   Lord god deliuer me.   24
>
>   Thow had to veritie sic zeill,
>   That of thy wisdome did reweill,
>   Incertane hid thingis for my weill,
>   And laid befoir myne E.   28

When I feel Thy grace I shall be whiter than snow.

>   For quhen thy fowth of grace I feill
>   I sal be clengit clene as steill,
>   And quhyttar than the snaw gret deill;
>   Lord god deliuer me.   32
>
>   Thow sall gif glaidnes vnto heir,
>   Me in to joy and mirthfull cheir,
>   Quhen all my febill bonis efeir
>   Sall gif the lovingis hie. 36

[lf. 17, p. 93]
Gaze not on my sins.

>   Heirfoir avart thy visage cleir,
>   So that my synnis cum not the neir;
>   Off my misdeidis quhilk dois me deir.
>   Lor[d] god deliuer me.   40
>
>   Creat within me and infound
>   Ane hart immaculat and mound,
>   Ane steidfast hairt renew and ground
>   Within my breist to be.   44

Chase me not from Thy face;

>   Fleme me nocht fra thy face fecound,
>   Bot lat thy haly spreit abound;
>   Lord god deliuer me.   48

let me rejoice in my salvation,

>   Restoir me to the exultatioun
>   I had in the of my saluatioun,
>   And with thy spreit of cheif probatioun
>   Anix sovirlie.   52

and I shall lead the wanderers to consolation.

>   I sall to synnaris mak narratioun,
>   And wicket men in deviatioun,
>   I sall thame ken to consolatioun.
>   Lord god deliuer me.   56

Lord God deliuer me, and gyd — Deliver me from shedding blood.
Frome schedding blude, and homicyd;
My tung sall preiss the just, but pryd,
          And petefull, all thre. 60
Lowse thow my lippis, that tyme and tyd — Let me praise Thee.
I may gif to the lovingis wyd,
Till all þat fermely list confyd.
          Lord god deliuer me. 64

Knew I thow covet sacrifyiss, — I would offer a sacrifice;
Or offerand holocast wald pryiss,
I sowld thame gif, bot thow dennyiss
          Sic to ressaif in gre; 68
For thy oblatioun, Lord, it lyiss — but a humble heart is Thy oblation.
In humill hairt, contreit alwyiss;
Pennens of spreit thow nolt dispyiss;
          Lord god deliuer me. 72

Sweit lord, to syon be suave, — [leaf 17 b, p. 94]
And strenth the wallis of thy conclave,
Jerusalem, thy haly grave,
          Quhilk makis ws ransone fre. 76
This sacrifice than thow salt have
Off thy just pepill, and ressave
Thair laill trew hairtis with all the lave,
          Lord god deliuer me. 80

Gloir to the fader he aboif, — Glory to Father, Son, and Holy Spirit.
Gloir to the sone for our behoif,
Gloir to the haly spreit of loif,
          In trenefald vnitie: 82
As wes, Is, Sal be ay, bot roif,
Ane thre, and thre in ane, to proif
Thy Godheid nevir may remoif:
          Lord god deliuer me. 84

The Wryttar to the Redare.

Heir endis this buik, written in tyme of pest,
Quhen we fra labor was compeld to rest,
Into the thre last monethis of this yeir,
From our Redemaris birth, to knaw it heir,
Ane thowsand is, ffyve hundreth, thre scoir awcht :
Of this purpois na mair it neidis be tawcht.
Swa, till conclude, God grant ws all gude end,
And eftir deth eternal lyfe ws send.
                                          [George Bannatyne.]

NOTES AND ILLUSTRATIONS.

Queen Mary received other poetical offerings besides that of Alexander Scott; the following verses were addressed to her by Sir Richard Maitland.

OF THE QUENIS ARRYVALL IN SCOTLAND.

Excellent Princes! potent, and preclair,
    Prudent, peerles in bontie and bewtie!
Maist nobil Quein of bluid under the air!
With all my hairt, and micht I welcum the
    Hame to thy native pepill, and cuntrie.
Beseikand God to gif the grace to haive
    Of thy leigis the hairtis faythfullie,
And thame in luife, and favour to receave.

Now sen thow art arryvit in this land,
    Our native Princes, and illuster Queine!
I traist to God this regioune sall stand
Ane auld frie land, as it lang tyme has bein.
    Quhairin, richt schoone, thair sall be hard and seine
Grit joy, justice, gude peax, and policie:
    All cair and cummer, baneist quyte and clein;
And ilk man leif in guid tranquillitie.

I am nocht meit nor abill, forthe to set
    How thow sall use discreitlie all thing heir:
Nor of ane Princes the dewtie and the det,
Quhilk I beleif thy heichnes hes perqueir.
    Bot, gif neid be, thair is anow can leir
Thy majestie, of thy awin natioune;
    And gif the counsall how to rewle and steir,
With wysdome all belangand to thy crowne.

Yet I exhort thè to be circumpect
    Of thy counsall in the electioune:
Cheis faythfull men of prudence and effect,
Quha will for wrang mak dew correctioune;
    And do justice, without exceptioune;
Men of knawledge, gude lyfe, and conscience
    That will nocht failye for affectioune,
Bot of gude fame, and lang experience

Quhilk, gif thow do, I hope that thow sall ring
    Lang in this land in grit felicitie.
Will thow pleis God, he will the send all thing
Is neidful to mantein thy royaltie;
    Quha gife thé grace to guyde sa prudentlie,

That all thy doing be to his plesour,
    And of Scotland to the commoditie,
Quilk, under God, thow hes now in thy cure.

And gif thy Hienes plesis for to marie,
    That thow haive help I pray the Trinitie
To cheis and tak ane husband without tarie
To thy honour, and our utilitie;
    Quha will, and may, mantein our libertie,
Repleit of wisdome and of godlienes;
    Nobill, and full of constance and lawtie;
With guid successioune, to our quyetnes.

Madam, I wes trew servand to thy Mother,
    And in hir favour stude ay thankfullie,
Of my estait als weill as ony other:
Prayand thy grace I may resavit be
    In siklyk favour with thy Majestie;
Inclynand ay to me thy gracious eiris;
    And, amang other servandis, thinke on me:
This last requeist I lernit at the freiris.

And thoch that I to serve be nocht sa abill
    As I wes wont, becaus I may not see;
Yet in my hairt I sall be firme and stabill
To thy Hienes, with all fidelitie;
    Ay prayand God for thy prosperitie;
And that I heir thy pepill, with hie voce,
    And joyful hairt, cryand continuallie,
Vive Marie tres-nobill Royne d'Escoss.

                 Sir Richard Maitland of Lethingtoun,
                     Poems, Ed. 1830, p. 16.

1/3. Queen Mary of Scotland was the daughter of James V. by Marie of Lorraine, the daughter of the Duke of Guise.

1/6. This line is very obscure. Hailes could not explain it. Perhaps it may mean welcome, "to beir the beill of our Albion," *i. e.* to take the lead in Scotland. There is a similar expression in John Rolland's *The Sevin Sages*, p. 238, edition 1837—

    . . . . . . luik than quha beiris the bell.

1/11. Great changes had taken place in the constitution of the Church at the time the poet was writing.

1/21. *trew kirk.* The Act of Parliament which disestablished the Roman hierarchy in Scotland was introduced and passed through all its stages on Aug. 24, 1560.

The Scottish parliament declared "that þe Jurisdictioun and autoritie of þe bischope of Rome callit þe paip, vsit within þis realme in tymes bipast, hes bene verray hurtful and preiudiciall to our soueranis autoritie and commone weill of þis realme. Thairfoir hes statute and ordanit that þe bischope of Rome haif na Jurisdictioun nor autoritie within þis realme in tymes cuming. And þat nane of oure said soueranis subiectis of þis realme sute or desire in ony tyme heireftir title or rycht be þe said bischope of Rome or his sait to ony thing within þis realme vnder þe panis of barratrye."

The poet speaks vaguely of the *trew kirk*, not wishing to offend the queen by condemning the Roman hierarchy; he ventures to express a hope that she will get a knowledge of the Gospel as taught in the *trew kirk*, by which he meant the reformed Church.

1/26. *force*, fortitude.

1/33. *cast thy consate* = regulate your plans. *caste* = determine, *consate* = thoughts, conceptions.

1/34. [who] *hes*. Scott very frequently allows the relative to be understood; see line 44 for another example.

1/44. After the reformation acts were passed, great struggles took place between the nobles for the possession of the Church lands.

1/45. Lord Hailes thinks that this is an allusion to the wanton destruction of ecclesiastical buildings of which the reformers in some cases were guilty.

1/49. The parliament of Henry VIII. had passed an act for the purpose of suppressing religious disputation; cf. 31 Henry VIII. cap. 14.

1/57. In the poems of Sir David Lindsay will be found many attacks on the licentiousness of the clergy.

1/65. The bastards of the higher clergy were considered good matches on account of their wealth. Lindsay, in *Ane Satire*, 4281, etc., suggested that if a nobleman married a priest's bastard daughter (the son of Lord Lindsay married a daughter of Cardinal Beatoun), he should be degraded and not be allowed to resume his dignities until he had been pardoned by the civil power; cf. Chalmers' Ed. of Sir D. Lindsay's works.

Lord Hailes says "the clergy were ambitious of giving their spurious daughters in marriage to men of family. It would be invidious to enter into particulars. Those who are acquainted with the history of Scotland need not be told that the best blood of the nation was contaminated by such base mixtures."

In a note on one of Dunbar's Poems, the 'General Satyre,' Hailes gives the following details:—"David Bethune, Abbot of Aberbrothock in 1525, afterwards Archbishop of St. Andrew's, and a cardinal under the title of Sancti Stephani in Cœlis Monte, had three bastards legitimated in one day; *Rec.*, b. 26, No. 330; William Stewart, Bishop of Aberdeen from 1532 to 1545, had a bastard son legitimated; *ibid.*, b. 28, No. 360, William Chisholme, Bishop of Dumblane from 1527 to 1564, gave great portions to his bastard son and two bastard daughters; Keith, *Catalogue of Scottish Bishops*, p. 105. Alexander Stewart, Bishop of Moray from 1527 to 1534, had a bastard daughter legitimated; *Rec.*, b. 30, No. 116: and a bastard son legitimated; *ibid.*, b. 30, No. 374. But they were all excelled by Patrick Hepburn, Bishop of Moray from 1535 until the Reformation, for he had five bastard sons all legitimated in one day; *ibid.*, b. 30, No. 585: and two bastard daughters, b. 30, No. 572."—*Ancient Scottish Poems*, 1770, pages 249 and 309.

The celibacy of the clergy was much denounced in popular ballads.

> God send euerie Priest ane wyfe,
>   And euerie Nunne ane man,
> That thay micht leue that haly lyfe,
>   As first the Kirk began.

> Sanct Peter, quhome nane can reprufe,
>   His lyfe in mariage led:
> All gude priestis quhome God did lufe,
>   Thair maryit wyfis had.

> Greit cause than, I grant, had they,
>   Fra wyfis to refraine :
> Bot greiter causis haue thay may
>   Now wyfis to wed againe.
>
> For than suld nocht sa mony hure
>   Be vp and downe this land ;
> Nor zit sa mony beggeris pure
>   In kirk and mercat stand.
>
> And nocht sa mekill bastard seid
>   Throw out this cuntrie sawin ;
> Nor gude men vncouth fry suld feid,
>   And all the suith war knawin.
>
> Sen Christis law, and commoun law,
>   And Doctouris will admit,
> That Preistis in that rock suld draw,
>   Quha dar say contrair it.
>
> *The Gude & Godlie Ballates*, Ed. Laing, p. 165.

1/73. Lindsay of Pitscottie records (*History of Scotland*, ed. 1778, p. 236) that a priest named Norman Galloway was burnt for marrying.

1/74. On St. Paul's day, 1543, five men and a woman were arrested for heresy at Perth. One was charged with interrupting a friar preaching, and for discussing scripture : two others were charged with desecrating a statue of St. Francis by nailing ram's horns on the forehead and a cow's-tail to the buttocks of the figure, and with eating a goose on the previous Halloween. The woman was charged with not calling on the Virgin when in travail. The judges were the Earl of Arran, the Earl of Argyll, and other nobles and the Cardinal. The victims were condemned to death. *John Knox's Works*, Laing's ed., vol. I., p. 524.

1/84. *syne saif þair kin*, and by this means save their kindred.

1/85. *þame* apparently refers to the images of St. Blais and St. Boit.

1/90. Hailes, *Ancient Scottish Poems*, reads *daifit*—the MS. has "daisit"; "daifit" makes better sense.

1/97. Queen Mary had declared her intention to have mass celebrated. The delegates of the Scotch kingdom promised that she should be allowed the private exercise of the ceremonies of her faith (McCrie, *Life of John Knox*, 175), hence the circumspectness of the poet's reference to the mass.

1/100. *lyne* = line of life or conduct ; Faithfully bases their conduct on loyalty.

1/103. The general sense seems to be that the poet thinks that the queen ought to forbid all but theologians from discussing Church matters.

1/113. The statutes reforming the Scottish Church had been enacted the year before Mary's return to Scotland.

1/127. Lord Hailes inserts this line under passages not understood. There is an attempt at explaining the passage in *Jamieson's Scottish Dictionary*. The author makes *kuikis* a verb meaning "to use every art." On this assumption the line would mean this : Sic hypocritical Christianis kuikis [uses every art] to kis [live in intimacy] with Chanteris [the laymen who had seized church lands]. In the 1882 edition of *Alexander Scott* there is a suggestion from Prof. Skeat that the true reading is *Chauceris kuikis*. In the Manciples Prologue the cook is described as a *stinking swine* whose *cursed breth* infected the pilgrims. To kiss such a person would be a punishment. Dr. Cranstoun, in his edition of *Alexander Scott*, adopts this reading and quotes from Montgomerie:

> Thy scrows obscure are borrowed fra some buike;
> Fra Lindsay thou tooke; thou'rt Chaucers cuike,
> Ay lying like a ruike gif men wald not skar thee.
> *The Flyting*, lines 112, 114.

Mr. William Mackean in his modernized edition of *Scott's Poems*, 1887, thinks the sense is: "Such Christianis, not contant with impropriating the Church rents, are mean enough to try to do the same with the endowments of the poor singers." The meaning seems to be that the poet wishes that the hypocrites he has described should be punished in some way.

1/129. Old folk are kept away from the new faith by its greedy followers, whose only religion is to seize the Church property.

1/137. The poets continued to complain of the state of the poor in the reign of James VI., as can be seen from these verses from the Bannatyne MS.:

(1)

> Now is our king in tendir aige
> Chryst conserf him in his eild,
> To do justice bath to man and pege,
> That garris our land ly lang unteild;
> Thocht we do dowble pay thair wege,
> Pur commonis presently now ar peild,
> Thay ryd about in sik a rege
> Be frith, forrest, and feild.
>   With bow, bucklar, and brand:
> Lo, quhair thay ryd intill the ry
> The divill mot fane your company,
> I pray fro my heart trewly:
>   This said Johne Up-on-land.

(2)

> He that wes wont to beir the barrowis
> Betwixt the baik-hous and the brew-hous
> On twenty shilling now he tarrowis,
> To ryd the he gait by the plewis:
> But wer I a king, and haif gud fallowis,
> In Norroway thay suld heir of newis;
> I suld him tak, and all his marrowis,
> And hing thame hich upon yone hewis,
>   And thairto plichtis my hand:
> Thir lordis and barronis grit,
> Upown ane gallows suld I knit,
> That thus down treddit has our quhit
>   Thus said Johne Up on land.

(3)

> Wald the lordis the lawis that leidis,
> To husbands do gud ressone and skill,
> To chaft anis thir chiftanis be the heidis,
> And hing thame heich vpoun ane hill;
> Than mycht husbandis labour thair steids,
> And preistis mycht pattir and pray thair fill;
> For husbands suld nocht haif sic pleids.
> Baith scheip and nolt[1] mycht ly full still   [1 cattle]

And stakis still myght stand:
For sen they red amang our durris
With splent on spald, and rousty spurris,
Thair grew no frutt intill our furris:
 Thus said Johne Up on land.

(4)
Tak a pur man a scheip or two
For hungir, or for falt of fude
To five or sex wie bairnis, or mo,
Thay will him hing with raipis rud;
Bot and he tak a flok or two,
A bow of ky, and lat thame blud,
Full falsly may he ryd or go:
I wait nocht gif thir lawis be gud.
 I schrew thame first thame fand.
Jesu, for thy holy passioun,
Thou grant him grace that weiris the crown,
To ding thir mony kingis doun:
 This said Johne Up on land.

1/141. "Cor mundum crea in me, Deus, et spiritum rectum innova in visceribus meis."—Ps. L. 12 (Vulgate). This text is often referred to in the poets of Scott's time. In "*The answer Quhilk Schir David Lyndesay maid to the Kingis flyting*," line 20, it occurs, "Quharefor, cor mundum crea in me, I cry."

1/142. *meir* is used as equivalent to "all a man's property or dues." "gif þe man his meir": "his meir" is used for "his due." There is a similar saying put in the mouth of Peter Bridgeward in Sir Walter Scott's *The Abbot* (chap. 16), when two retainers wish to cross the bridge without paying. "Come Papist, come Protestant, ye are all the same. The Papist threatened us with Purgatory, and fleeched us with pardons—the Protestant smits at us with his sword, and cuittles us with the liberty of conscience; but never a one of either says, 'Peter, there is your penny.'" In *Rob Roy* (chap. 32) the phrase occurs, "Gie the honest man his mear again," in the same sense as in the poem.

1/145. *auld antetewme*, give, give, give. John Knox denounced the Protestant nobles for their greed in seizing the Church property. Their view of Knox is expressed by Sir Walter Scott in *The Abbot* (Centenary ed., p. 213), by these words put in the mouth of the Regent Morton, "Here is John Knox, who made such a noble puller-down, is ambitious of becoming a setter-up, and a founder of schools and colleges out of the Abbey lands and bishops rents, and other spoils of Rome, which the nobility of Scotland have won with their sword and bow, and with which he would endow new hives to sing the old drone."

Knox's opinion of the nobility may be seen in his history; this extract will indicate it: "Some approved it [The Book of Discipline] and willed the samyn have bene sett furth be a law. Otheris perceaving thair carnall libertie and wordlie commoditie some what to be impaired thairby, grudged insomuche that the name of the Book of Discipline became odious unto thame. Everie thing that repugned to thair corrupt affectionis was termed mockage, 'devote imaginationis." The caus we have befoir declaired; some war licentious; some had greadelie gripped to the possessionis of the kirk; and otheris thought that thei wald nott lack thair parte of Christis coat; yea, and that befoir that ever he was hanged, as by the Preachearis thei war oft rebuked. The cheaf great man that had professed Christ Jesus, and refuissed to subscrive the Book of Discipline, was the Lord Erskyn; and no wonder, for besydis that he has a verray Jesabell to his wyffe. Yf the poore, the schooles, and the ministrie of the kirk had thair awin his keching [kitchen] wald lack two parttis and more, of that whiche he injustlie now possesses. Assuredlye some of us have woundered how men that professe godlynes could of so long continewance hear the threatnyngis of God against theavis and against thair housses, and knowing thame selfis guyltie in suche thingis, as war open rebucked, and that thei never had remorse of conscience, neather yitt intended to restore any thingis of that, whiche long thei had stollen and reft. Thair was none within the Realm more unmercyfull to the poore Ministeris than war thei whiche had greatest rentis of the churches. But in that we have perceaved the old proverbe to be trew, "Nothing can suffice a wreche," and agane "The bellie hes none earis." *History of the Reformation*, Book III.

To the same effect are these lines by Sir Richard Maitland, who wrote about the same time as Alexander Scott, *Pinkerton's Ancient Scottish Poems*, vol. ii., 324.

>   Sum comouns, that hes bene weill stakit
>   Under kirkmen, ar now all wrakit,
>   Sen that the teynd and the kirk landis
>   Came in grit temporale mennis handis.
>   Thai gar the tennents pay sic sowmes
>   As thai will ask, or quha ganestandis
>   Thai will be put sone fra thair rowmes.
>
>   The teynd, quhilk tennents had befoir
>   Of thair awin malingis, corne and stoir,
>   Thair laird hes tane it our thair heid,
>   And gars thame to his yaird it leid:
>   Bot thair awin stok thai dar not steir
>   Thoch all thair bairnis sould want breid
>   Quhill thai have led that teynd ilk yeir.
>
>   Sic extorsioun and taxatioun
>   Wes never sene into this natioun,
>   Tane of the comouns of this land;
>   Of quhilk sum is left waist liand,
>   Becaus few may sic chairgis beir.
>   Mony hes quhips now in thair hand
>   That wont to have bayth jak and speir.

1/153. 1 Corinthians, x. 14, "Wherefore, my beloved, flee from idolatry."

1/156. þat leud burd-lyme, covetousness; cf. l. 118.

1/195. These lines were ascribed to Thomas the Rhymer. There are other verses in *Ancient Scottish Prophecies* to somewhat the same effect by Berlington. Sir Walter Scott, *Minstrelsy of the Scottish Border*, thinks these prophecies were fabricated about 1515 to support the Duke of Albany, the regent of Scotland, who came from France two years after the fatal field of Flodden. They had great currency in Scotland, and were regarded as authentic by learned men in the seventeenth century, like Archbishop Spottiswood, the author of the *History of the Church of Scotland;* see p. 47 of the *History*, 1677 ed.

THE PROPHECIE OF BERTLINGTON.

How euer it happen for to fall,
The¹ Lyon shal be Lord of all. [¹ *i.e.* Scotch]
the Frenche wife shall beare the Sonne,
Shal weild al Bretane to the sea,
and from the Bruces blood shall come
As neere as the ninth degree,
Meruelous Merling that many men of tells,
And Thomas sayings comes all at once,
Thogh their sayings be selcouth,
they shal be suith found
and there shal all our glading be,
The crow shal sit vpon a stone,
and drinke the gentle blood so free.

Take of the ribes and beare to her birdes,
As God hath said so must it be.
Then shal Ladies laddes wed,
And brooke Castles and Towers hie.
Beid hath breued in his booke, and Banister also.
Meruelous Merling, and al accordes in one
Thomas the trew, that neuer spake false
Consents to their saying, and the same terme hath taken,
Yet shall there come a keene knight ouer the salt sea.
a keene man of courage, and bolde man of armes,
A Dukes sonne doubled, a borne man in France
That shal our mirthes amend, and mend all our harms
After the date of our Lord, 1513, and thrise three there after,
Which shal brooke al the braid Ile to him selfe
Betwix XXIII, and thrise three the Threip shal be ended.
the saxons shal neuer recouer after
He shal be crowned in the kith, in the Castle of Douer,
Which weares the Golden Garland of Iulius Cesar.
More worship shal he win of greater worth,
Than euer Arthur himselfe had in his daies,
Many doughtie deedes shal he doe there after,
Which shal be spoken of many dayes better.

From R. Waldegraue's edition of 1603.

1/196.   Or who shall rule the Isle of Britane
From the north to the south sey ?
A French queen shall beare the sonne
Shall rule all Britaine to the sea,
Which of the Bruces blood shall come
As neere as the nynt degree.

Ancient Scottish Prophecies, printed by Andro Hart, 1615.

1/197. The following is the pedigree of Mary Stuart :—

0. Robert Bruce, *d.* 1329; *m.* Isabella, daughter of Donald, 10th Earl of Mar.

1. Marjory, *d.* 1316; *m.* Walter, the High Steward, *d.* 1327.

2. Robert II, *b.* 1316, *d.* 1370; *m.* (1) Elizabeth Mure, (2) Euphemia, daughter of Earl of Ross.

3. Robert III, b. ? 1340, d. 1406; m. Anabell Drummond.

4. James I, b. 1394, d. 1437; m. Jeane, daughter of John, Duke of Somerset.

5. James II, b. 1430, d. 1460; m. Marie, daughter of Arnold, Duke of Geldre.

6. James III, b. 1451, d. 1488; m. Margaret of Denmark.

7. James IV, b. 1473, d. 1513; m. Margaret of England.

8. James V, b. 1512, d. 1542; m. Marie, Duchess of Longeville, daughter of the Duke of Guise.

9. Mary Queen of Scots, b. 1542, d. 1587; m. (1) Francis II, King of France, d. 1560; m. (2) Henry, Earl of Darnley, d. 1567; m. (3) James Hepburn, Earl of Bothwell, d. 1569.

2/title. The Drum is a mansion not far from Edinburgh; it is now known as Somerville House. It was the seat of the Somervilles. In 1584, some years after this poem was written, Hugh, the seventh Lord Somerville, who married a daughter of the fifth Lord Seton, had a mansion built by John Milne, the King's master builder. This house lasted until the end of last century, when it gave place to the present building. The estate passed into the hands of the Somervilles in the 14th century. They sold it in the year 1800. The grounds round the mansion were celebrated for their beauty.

2/8. A reference to the twelfth labour of Hercules, which consisted of securing the many-headed dog Cerberus, who guarded the portals of the infernal regions, and dragging him up on earth.

2/56. *sidder* = ? to place in position.

2/68. "Bound himself by a vow to the peacock, according to the usual custom of knights upon their undertaking to give some conspicuous proof of their valour."—Sibbald, *Chronicle of Scottish Poetry*, III. 143.

Knights used to make vows by the swan, the heron, and the pheasant, as well as by the peacock.

2/156. "keild." Mackean reads "keeled," *pp.* of "keel," to mark with red earth. Edinburgh boys speak of "keeling a laddie," *i.e.* putting a chalk mark on a boy's back. The term is generally applied to marking sheep. Although "keild" is used in line 26, meaning killed, here "keeling" would be sufficient punishment for the cowardice of Will, and more in the spirit of the verse.

3/10. *to play vpcoill with the bawis.* "This seems to refer to the ancient customs of tossing up different balls into the air and catching them before they reached the ground." Jamieson's *Scot. Dict.*, ed. 1882, IV. 675.

3/13. *Hunts vp*, a popular Scotch song: see *The Complaynt of Scotland*, E. E. T. S. ed., p. 66; it is also mentioned by Henrysun:

"The cadgear sang Hunts vp, vp, vpon hie."

Semple refers to it in the 'Piper of Kilbarchan,' and Adamson in the *Muses Threnodie* speaks of it.

"Courage to give was mightilie then blown
Saint Johnston's hunts vp since then most famous known
By all musitians when they sweetlie sing
With heavenly voice and well concording string."

Joseph Ritson, *Dissertation on Ancient Songs and Music*, on the authority of Puttenham, says the song was composed in the time of Henry VIII. by William Gray, and quotes a verse of the song:

> "The hunt is vp, the hunt is vp,
> And now it is almost day,
> And he that's in bed with another man's wife,
> It's time to get him away."

Chappell says that any song intended to arouse in the morning, even a love-song, was formerly called "A hunt's up."

The following parody of the song of *Hunts Vp* throws light on the state of feeling among some of the opponents of Catholicism in Scotland.

1

With huntis vp, with huntis vp,
It is now perfite day,
Jesus, our King, is gane hunting,
Quha lykis to speid thay may.

2

Ane cursit fox lay hid in rox
This lang and mony ane day,
Deuouring sheip, quhill he micht creip,
Nane micht him schaip away.

3

It did him gude to laip the blude
Of young and tender lammis;
Nane culd he mis, for all was his,
The ȝoung anis with thair dammis.

4

The hunter is Christ, that huntis in haist,
The hundis ar Peter and Paull,
The Paip is the foxe, Rome is the rox
That rubbis vs on the gall.

5

That cruell beist, he neuer ceist,
Be his vsurpit power,
Under dispens to get our penneis,
Our saulis to deuoir.

6

Quha culd deuyse sic merchandise
As he had thair to sell,
Onles it war proud Lucifer,
The greit maister of Hell.

7

He had to sell the Tantonie[1] bell, [1 *Bell of St. Anthony.*]
And pardonis thairin was
Remissioun of Sinnis in auld sheip skinnis
Our saulis to bring from grace

8

With bullis of leid, quhyte wax and reid,
And vther quhylis with grene,
Closit in ane box, this vsit the fox,
Sic peltrie[2] was neuer sene.   [2 *pedlar's trash.*]

9
With dispensatiounis and obligatiounis
  According to his law,
He wald dispens, for money from hence,
  With thame he neuer saw.

10
To curs and ban the sempill pure man,
  That had nocht to flé the paine ;
But quhen he had payit all to ane myte,
  He mon be absoluit than

11
To sum, God wot, he gaue tot quot
  And vther sum pluralitie ;
Bot first with penneis he mon dispens
  Or ellis it will not be.

12
Kingis to marie, and sum to tarie,
  Sic is his power and micht,
Quha that hes gold, with him will he hold,
  Thocht it be contrair all richt.

13
O blissit Peter, the foxe is ane leir,
  Thow knawis weill it is nocht sa,
Quhill at the last, he salbe downe cast
  His peltrie, pardonis, and all.

"Ane Cōpendious buik of godlie Psalms and Spirituall Sangis collectit furthe of sindrie partis of the Scripture, with diueris vtheris Ballatis Changeit out of prophane sangis in godlie Sangis, for auoyding of sin and harlatrie."—Edinburgh, 1578.

There is another religious parody of the song at end of Halliwell's *Wit and Science.*

3/17. The representation of Robin Hood and Little John was in full swing in 1508, as appears from an entry dated May 8th of that year, in proceedings of the City of Aberdeen Council. "The said day it was statut and ordanit be the alderman, baillies, and counsale, that all persons that ar abill within this burghe salbe reddy with their arrayment maid in grene and yallow, bowis, arrowis, brass, and all uther convenient thingis according thairto, to pass with Robyne Huyd and Litile Johnne, all tymes convenent tharto, quhen thai be requirit be the said Robyne Huyd and Litile Johnne, eftir the tenor of the statuts and proclamatioun maid be the proveistis, baillis, and counsaill ; and gif ony of the said personis happenis to failye in ony poynt befor writyne [he] sall pay fourty shillings unforgiven, and sall noch bruik nor joiss tak, fisching, nor land of the said burgh." Another entry is dated 17 Nov., 1508: "The said day, the prouest, bailyeis, counsaill, and comunitie of the said burghe, representand the haill body of the samyne warnit be the hand bell, ale in ane voice considerand, riplie avisit, for the auld rit and lovabile consuetud of the said burgh, vsit and perseurit all tymes bigane, past memor of man, in the honor of thar glorius patron Sanct Nicholaice, statut and ordanit, that all personis, burges, nichtbouris, and inhabitaris, burges sonnys habyll to ryd, to decor and honor the towne in thar array conveinant therto, sall rid with Robert Huyid and Litile Johne, quhilk was callit, in yers bipast, Abbat and Prior of Bonacord, one every sanct

SCOTT.   G

Nicholas day, throw the towne, as use and wont has bene, quhen thai wer warnit be the said Robert Huyde or Litile Johne, or ony ane of theme; and giff ony man haffand taks of watris, fischeingis, landis, or ony pensioun or proffit of the toune, habill to rid, beand warnit be the saidis Robert Huyd or Litile Johne forsaid, and will nocht ryd, and beis convict tharintill be ane suorne assiss of the said burgh, [thai] sall tyne thar takis, pensiounis, and proffitis that thai haue of the said burghe, and sal be secludit, removit, and uterlie expellit fra all takis, pensionis, proffits, quhatsumever thai have of the said burgh, in tyme to cum; without ressonable causs schawin and propinit to the prouest, bailyeis, counsaill, Robene and Litile Johne, obefoir, and be considert be thame to be lauchfull impediment and excuss quharthrow thai mycht not ryd; and the personis havand na takis of the said burghe, beand warnit be the said Robert Huyd or Litile Johnne, and will not rid, sall pay xx shillings [1/8] to Sanct Nicholas werk, and viij sh [8 pence] to the bailyeis unlaw vnforgetin."

On the 30th April, 1535, there was a provision made for suitable green coats being provided for the representation of Robin Hood: "The said day, it is thocht expedient, and ordanit be the consale, that all the young able men within this guid toun, have their grene cottis; and agit men, cottis efferand to thame; and obey and decor the Lordis of Bonaccord, conform to the auld lovable vse of this guid tovn, under the painis of braking of commands and statutis of the guid toun, that beis convickit tharof, and to be punest conform tharto." It would appear from the statute of April 13, 1552, that the pastime caused great extravaugance: "The said day, the counsell, all in ane voce, havand respect and consideratioune that the Lordis of Bonacord, in tymis bigan, hes maid our mony grit, sumpteous, and superfluous banketing, induring the tyme of thair regnne, and speciallie in May, quhilke wes thocht nother profitabill nor godlie, and did hurt to sindry young personis that wer elekit in the sad office, becaus thae last elekit did ay pretend to surmont on thair predecessoris, in ryetouss and sumpteous banketing, and the causs, princpall, and gud institutioun thairof, quilk wes inhalding of the guid toun in glaidnes and blythnes with danssis, farsiss, playis, and gamis in tymes convenient, [wes] neclekit and abusit: Thairfoir ordanis that in tyme cuming, all sic sumpteous bankating be laid doun aluterlie; except thre sober and honest [bankats], viz. wpoun the Seyne day [Ascension Day]; the first Sonday of May; and ane uthir upoun Tuiseday efter Pasche day [Good Friday]; and na honest man to pass to ony of thair bankeitis, except on the said thre dais allanerlie; and in the place of the forsaid superfluous banketting, to be had and maid yeirly twa plais, or ane at the lest, with danssis and games usit and wont; quhasaiver refuisis to accept the said office, in tym cuming, beand elekit tharto be the toun, to tyne his fredome privilege, takis, and profitt he hes, or may haf, of the toun, and never to be admittit frathinsfurth, to office, honor nor dignitie."

The representations of Robin Hood and Little John were forbidden by statute in 1551, as they were the occasions of disorder. The people were loath to give up their favourite amusement, and after the Reformation these representations were taken advantage of to ridicule Roman Catholicism. In June 1555 another Act was passed: Item, It is statute and ordanit that in all tymes cumming na maner of persoun be chosen, Robert Hude nor Lytill Johne Abbot of vnressoun, Quenis of May, nor vtherwyse nouther in Burgh, nor to landwart in ony tyme to cum. And gif ony Prouest, Baillies, counsall, and communitie chesis sic ane Personage as Robert Hude Lytill Johne Abbottis of vnressoun, or Quenis of Maij within

Notes and Illustrations. 83

Burgh, the chesaris of sic sall tyne thair fredome for the space of fyue ȝeiris, and vtherwyse salbe punist at the Quenis grace will, and the acceptar of siclyke office salbe banist furth of the Realme. And gif ony sic persounis sic as Robert Hude Lytill Johne Abbottis of vnressoun, Quenis of Maij beis chosin outwith, Burgh and vthers landwart townis the chesaris sall pay to our Souerane Lady X. pundis and thair persounis put in waird thair to remane during the Quenis grace plesoure. And gif ony wemen or vthers about simmer treis singand, makis perturbation to the Quenis liegis in the passage throw Burrowis and vthers landwart townis the wemen perturbatowis for skafrie[1] of money or vtherwyse salbe takin, handellit, and put vpone the Cukstulis of euerie Burgh or towne.

In Knox's *History of the Reformation*, Guthrie's ed., p. 244, there is an account of a serious riot in Edinburgh in 1561, in consequence of a revival of Robin Hood; as late as 1592 the General Assembly of the Kirk of Scotland complained that the Sabbath was profaned by representations of Robin Hood. For a description of these dramas see Sir Walter Scott's *The Abbot*, chaps. xiv. and xv.

3/20. *clown robbynis;* "clown" seems the better reading, though the MS. may be read *clovin*. *Robbynis* I take as meaning rustics, cf. Henryson's *Robene* and *Makyne*, though Jamieson, *Scot. Dict.*, says it means either ruffians, or bankrupts.

3/21-25. The meaning of the stanza is very obscure. In Jamieson's *Scottish Dictionary* it is suggested that it is a reference to the disordered state of the times. Lawless abbots and lords, *i. e.* not mummers, but real disturbers of the commonwealth, are unfortunately in evidence in other months besides May. Possibly Scott had in view the riots in 1561 over the play of Robin Hood. In that year the Edinburgh populace organized, in spite of the statute referred to above, the game of Robin Hood. The baillies tried to suppress the demonstration without success. There was much disturbance, and during the hubbub the roughs committed various robberies. The magistrates arrested one, James Gillon; he was charged with robbery, convicted, and sentenced to death: but the populace broke into the Tolbooth where the convict was confined, and liberated him as well as all the other prisoners. The riot did not stop until the Provost and Baillies gave "their handwrits, that they should never pursue any of them that were of the tumult, for any crime that was done in that behalf."—Knox's *History of the Reformation* (Guthrie's ed., 1898), p. 246.

3/24. *fibilnes*, perhaps the true reading is *fikilnes*.

3/30. In the latter part of May: the sun passes from Taurus to Gemini about the 21st of May, and continues in it till about June 21st.

3/41. The following Acts of Parliaments show the efforts of the Scotch government to promote archery.

Item, it is ordanyt þat all men busk þame to be archares fra þei be xij ȝeres of eilde. And þat in ilk x ti worth of lande þar be maid bowmerkes, and specialy ner' paroche kirkes, quhar' vpone haly dais men may cum, and at þe lest schute thriss about and haif vsage of archary. And quha sa vsis no[t] þe said archary þe lord of the lande sal raiss of him a wedder, and gif þe lorde raiss no[t] þe saide payne þe kingis schiref or his ministers sall raiss it to þe King.—James I, A.D. 1424, Cap. 19.

Item, it is decretyt and ordanyt þat wapinschawingis be haldin be þe lordis ande baronys, spirituale and temperale, four tymis in þe ȝer'. And at þe fut ball and þe golf be vtterly criyt done and no[t] vsyt. Ande at þe

[1] Extortion.

bowe markis be maide at ilk paroch kirk a pair of buttis and schuting be vsyt ilk sunday, And þat ilk man schut sex schottis at the lest vnder þe payne to be raisit apone thame þat cumis not at the lest ijd to be giffin to þame þat cumis to þe bowe markis to drink. And this to be vsyt fra pasche till alhallomess efter. And be þe nixt mydsomer to be reddy with all þer graith without failȝe. And that þer be a bowar and a fleger in ilk hede towne of þe schyr. And þat þe towne furnyss him of stuf and graithe efter as nedes him þerto þat he may serve the cuntre with. And as tuichande þe futball and þe golf we ordane it to be punyst be þe baronys vnlawe. And gif he takes not the vnlaw that it be takin be þe kingis officiaris. Ande gif þe perochin be mekill þat þer be iij or iiij of þe bow markis in sik placis as ganys þer for. And that ilk man within þat perochin that is within fyfte and passit xij ȝeris sall vse schuting, and þat men þat is outwith and past three scoir ȝeiris sal vse vþir honest gammys as efferis.—James II, 1457, Cap. 6. Laws to promote the practice of archery were passed in 1471, 1491, 1540.

Item, Tuiching þe first artikle anentis þe wapinshewin It Is thoycht necessare þat wapinschawingis be maid tuiss in þe ȝeir outthrow all þe realme, That Is to say, In the monethis of Junij And October, at sic day or dayis, and place as sall pleiss þe Schereff, stewart, ballies, prouestis, aldermen of burrowis Till assigne aftir þe quantitie of þe schire, gif þe moustouris cañnot be all tane on ane day. And þat þai mak warningis þer to vpoun þe prem[on]itioun of xx dais, And at þe saidis munstouris be tane be þe schireff of þe schire prouest and balȝeis of burrowis and balȝeis of regaliteis, and vþer comissaris quheme þe kingis grace plesis to assigne to þame, And becaus þai haif bene sa lang out of vse of making of wapingschawing It is Thot expedient þat þe samin be maid thrise for þe first ȝeire, And þe first tyme to be oñ þe morne eftir laif Sounday nixt to cum. —James V, Dec. 1540, Cap. 21.

3/44. "*reveris*" and "*prikkis*." "The marks usually shot at by the archers for pastime were 'butts, prickes, and roavers.' The butt, we are told, was a level mark, and required a strong arrow, with a very broad feather; the pricke was a 'mark of compass,' but certain in its distance; and to this mark strong swift arrows, of one flight, with a middling sized feather were best suited; the roaver was a mark of uncertain length; it was therefore proper for the archer to have various kinds of arrows, of different weights, to be used according to the different changements made in the distance of the ground."—T. Strutt's *Sports and Pastimes*, London, 1810, p. 56.

3/45. Perhaps the correct reading is "Sum laich and lo[w] beneth the clais." *Clais*. Cotgrave gives *claye* = a hurdle of osiers. *Clais* were probably hurdles placed on either side of the butts to intercept arrows that happened to go wide of the mark.

3/53. *bairis*. Probably the game of Prisonirs Bars as described in Strutt's *Sports and Pastimes*, p. 59.

3/54. *barlabreikis*. A game played in a cornyard. A stack is made the dule or goal. The players assemble round the stack: one is made the catcher, the others run away and hide. The catcher tries to capture the players, while they try to avoid this by running back to the stack. Those who are caught away from the stack have to help to catch the other players. When all get to the stack or are caught, the game begins again; the first player who was made prisoner having to play the part of catcher. Cf. Jamieson's *Scot. Dict.*

"At barleybraiks we laughin' chased ilk kimmer we could see."
Robert Nicoll's Poems.

3/55. Probably this means the game of tig or touch. Some run round about the standing pillars playing at tig.

3/56. *Lareit.* At the east end of Musselburgh was the celebrated chapel of Our Lady of Loretto with the Hermit's Cell adjoining; during the ravages of the Earl of Hertford, in May 1544, he destroyed this famous chapel, and a part of the Town: it was soon repaired, but it was finally abolished at the Reformation, and in 1590 the materials of the chapel which had once so many votaries, were converted to the building of the Tolbooth of Musselburgh. This is said to have been the first Religious House in Scotland, whose ruins were applied to an unhallowed use, for which the good people of Musselburgh are said to have been annually excommunicated until very lately at Rome."—Nicholas Carlisle's *Topographical Dictionary of Scotland,* London, 1813.

"Of the chapel of Lorretto.... nothing remains but a small burial vault; and a thick grove now usurps the bank where votaries knelt at the shrine of Mary Magdalene."—*The New Statistical Account of Scotland,* 1845, vol. i. p. 271.

"Sir David Lindsay (*Ane Dialog betuix Experience and Ane Curteour*) condemned these pilgrimages to Loretto and the hermit because much mischief resulted from the promiscuous gathering of the youths of both sexes. James V. made a pilgrimage from Stirling to Loretto in 1536 in order to procure a propitious passage to France where he was going to search for a wife. Cf. Chalmers' *Caledonia.* The Hermit was naturally an oponent of the reformation, and he was satirized by the Earl of Glencairn in the following verses."—Knox's *History of the Reformation,* ed. C. T. Guthrie, 1898.

AN EPISTLE DIRECTED FROM THE HOLY HERMIT OF ALAREIT
TO HIS BRETHREN THE GREY FRIARS.

I, Thomas, hermite in Larite,
Saint Francis' order do heartily greet,
Beseching you with firm intent,
To be walkryfe (*watchful*) and diligent;
For these Lutherians, risen of new,
Our Order daily do pursue.
These smaikis (*mean fellows*) do sent their haill intent,
To read the English New Testament.
They say, we have them clean disceavit;
Therefore in haste they maun be stoppit!
Our state, "hypocrisie" they prize (*reckon*),
And no blaspheamis on this wyse:
Saying, That we are heretikes,
And false, loud lying mastiff tykes,
Stout fishers with the Fiend's net,
The upclosers of Heaven's yett (*gate*)
Cankered corrupters of the Creed,
Hemlock-sowers amongst good seed,
Kirk men that are to Christ unkent,
A sect that Satan's self has sent!

. . . .

I dread this doctrine if it last,
Shall either gar (*make*) us work or fast;
Therefore, with speed we must provide
And not our profit overslide.

. . . . .

> Your Order handles no money,
> But for other casuality,
> As beef, meal, butter and cheese
> Or what else ye have, that ye please,
> Send your Brethern, et habete.
> As now nought else but valete.
>> By Thomas your brother at command,
>> A cullurne kythed (*silly fellow exhibited*) through many a land.

3/58. *To horss.* This probably means to assist them to mount on horseback.

3/65. *thankless mowth.* The same image is used by Sir David Lindsay "Answer to Kingis Flyting," l. 33, for "pudenda muliebria."

4/0. This poem was ascribed by David Laing to Alexander Scott in his edition of the poet's works. It was first printed by Chepman and Myllar in 1508, and consequently it must be by an earlier writer. The following is the version of the song in Forbes' *Cantus* (3rd ed. 1682), of the first four verses of this poem:

> Lusty May with Flora Queen,
> The balmy drops from Phebus sheen
> Prelusant beams before the day
> By thee Diana groweth green
> Through gladness of this lusty May (repeated).
>
> Then Aurora that is so bright
> To woful hearts he casts great light,
> Right plesantly before the day
> And shows and shads forth of that light
> Through gladness of this lusty May (repeated).
>
> Birds on their beughs of every sort
> Sends forth their notes and makes great mirth
> On banks that blooms on euery bray,
> And fares and flyes ov'r field and firth
> Through gladness of this lusty May (repeated).
>
> All Lovers hearts that are in care,
> To their Ladies they do repare,
> In fresh mornings before the day
> And are in mirth ay more and more
> Through gladness of this lusty May (repeated).
>
> [Of every moneth in the year,
> To mirthful May there is no peer;
> Her glistring garments are so gay,
> Your Lovers all, make merry cheer,
> Through gladness of this Lusty May.]

4/9. The weather is fine: April showers are out of sight.
5/1. Love oppresses without distinction.
5/8. Get mastery over.
5/14. This proverb occurs often in the Scotch poets:

> Thocht I in court be maid refus,
> And haif few vertewis for to rus;
> Yet am I cumin of Adame and Eif,

Notes and Illustrations. 87

And fane wald leif as uderis dois
Excess of thocht dois me mischeif.
William Dunbar: To the King, Stanza VIII.

5/20. *docht him dress* could give.
5/21, 22. Because to enjoy princely love is to have complete or express sovereignty.
5/23. Service comes from humility.
5/29. The same proverb occurs in A. Montgomerie's *The Cherrie and the Slae*, 1597:

Maire honor is, to vanquische ane,
Nor feicht with tensum, and be tane,
And outhir hurt or slane:
The prattick is, to bring to passe,
And not to enterprise;
And als guid drinking out of glas,
As gold in ony wise.

5/30. *at all devyss* = elaborately.
5/40. She may see some literary merit in it. The Scottish poets called their language Inglis, in contrast to the (supposed) rude and barbaric dialects of the Celtic population of Scotland. Dunbar in his 'Flyting with Kennedy' taunts him as being an Erse or Gaelic poet. Gaelic was then widely spoken over the N., the W., and S.-W. of Scotland.
6. Poem seven is Scott's answer to these lines.
7/12. *abone þe laif* = above all others.
7/27. *f. f.* = without falsehood.
7/30. *b. . . . r.* = unless you pity it.
7/35. *b. . . . i.* = unless you send it.
8/20. *at all* = altogether.
8/30. lustiest]. Irving, in *History of Scottish Poetry*, reads "lufliest." The MS. is somewhat indistinct.

The epithet, "lamp of ladies," is found in 1/218. It was used by Lindsay and others:

Fair weill! ye lemant lampis of lustines
Of fair Scotland, adew my Ladies all.
The Testament of Squyer Meldrum, stanza 33.

9/21. *I wiss* = certainly. A.S. *gewiss*.
9/23. There is nothing on earth I am anxious about.
9/27. *moif* = stir up, excite.
9/33. *done in fawouris* = got into favour.
10/1. I will be open, and love sincerely.
10/24. *ay quhill* = until.
10/27. *our cast* = cast over, reject.
11/4. *q. i.* = in whom.
11/10. *v. s.* = another one.
11/20, 21. Else know without more words that the dart of Cupid will pierce my heart.
11/23. *b. b.* = sorrows abate.
11/25. *c.* = ended.
11/28. *Quhill deid departe* = until death separates us.
11/33. That may me þat is pynd appeill fra my langour.
11/34. MS. reads *And to sla*; the *to* seems to be an error of the transcriber.
11/40. *plicht* = involved [in unsatisfied longings].
12/5. The cockatrice or basilisk, an imaginary creature which was fabled to kill by a look:

88   *Notes and Illustrations.*

> A cokatrice hast thou hatched to the world,
> Whose unavoided eye is murderous.
>   Shakespere, *Richard III*, IV. i. 55.

"By confusion with *cock*, it was said to be a monster hatched from a cock's egg; it is merely a perversion of *crocodile*."—Skeat's *Dictionary of English Language*.

12/12. *barrat* appears to mean any common worthless stone.

13/2. *in staige* = step by step.

13/4. *thirlaige* = in a state of servitude. The meaning is that he is free from any kind of servile bond. The word is a legal term, as are *heretaige* and *blenche-ferme* in the same stanza.

13/21. "lord" and l. 34, and "god," l. 27, refers to Cupid.

13/28. I bought her dear, but she bought me yet dearer, as she hazarded her honor and fame by the intrigue.

13/36. *s . . . e* leave without being seen.

13/38. *went* = wend, go.

14. This song is published in a volume, "Cantus, Songs and Fancies, I. Forbes, Aberdeen 1662." The transcript below of the song is from p. 11 of the edition (3rd) published in 1682, in the Advocates' Library, Edinburgh. The text has some variations from Bannatyne MS. The music below is the modernized version supplied in David Laing's edition of *Scott's Poems*, published 1821. The version from the Panmure MS., in the Library of the Earl of Dalkeith, is taken from Dr. Cranstoun's edition.

> For well I wot was never wight,
> That could inforce his mind & might
> To love and serve his Ladie bright,
>   and want her syne.
> As I do martyr day and night
> Without that onlie thing of right,
>   that should be mine.

Were I of puissance for to prove
My lowlie and my heartlie love,
I should her mind to mercie move
    With such propine.
Were all the world at my behove,
She should it have at here behove
    for to be mine.

Now whom to shal I make my moan?
For truth nor constancie is none;
For all the faithful love is gone
    Of feminine.
It would oppress an heart of stone
To see my loss, for her alone
    that should be mine.

Who shal my dulled spirits raise,
Since not for love my Ladie goes?
For if good service might her please
    She should incline.
I die in doulour and disease,
And others hath her as they please
    that should be mine.

I may perceive right well by this,
That all the blythness, joy and bliss,
The lustie wanton life I wish
    Of love is hine.
What remedie since so it is?
But patience, suppose I miss
    that should be mine.

For Nobles hath not ay renown,
Nor Gentles ay the gayest gown,
They carie victuals to the town
    that worse doth dine.
So busily to busk I bown,
And others beats the berry down
    that should be mine.

Who can the rage of youthhood daunt,
Let him to Lovers Court go haunt,
And him as Venus subject grant,
    and keep her trine.
Perchance he shal find mercy skant,
And able his reward not want
    as I do mine.

14/22. *q. t.* = to whom.
14/31. *B. a.* = But if.
14/44. *gayest.* Dr. Cranstoun prints *grayest*, probably a misprint.
14/48. *eitis.* The MS. has had a letter scraped out. The true reading may be *beitis*, as suggested by the Cantus version.
14/52. *tham... grant* = become subjects of Venus.
15. Between poems 14 and 15 the following stanza is found in the MS.

    Ane laid may lufe ane leddy of estait,
    Ane lord ane lass, lufe hes no vdir law.
    Quha can vndo that is predestinat,
    Oft syiss for lufe the lynnage lichtlis law,

Rycht as the sone schynis on the sudly schaw,
And eik the rane vpoun the ryall ross,
Sa oft tymis lufe cheissis ane vnlyk choiss.
[Anon.]

15/13. *w. . . . r.* = will not show pity on me.
15/20. Because by thee engraved.
15/23. *f.* = fail.
15/24. Little honour is it to spoil or injure her servant.

16. Lord Hailes suggests (notes to *Ancient Scottish Poems,* page 314) that the person referred to was Robert, Master of Erskine, eldest son of John, fourth Lord Erskine (and fifth Earl of Mar, who died in 1552) . . . He was killed at the battle of Pinkie Cleugh, 10th September 1547, without issue. John Knox, in his *History,* records that Mary of Lorraine, Queen-Dowager, made "grit lamentatioun" when she heard of his decease, "and bure his deythe mony dayis in mynd," because she "deirlie belovit" him ; cf. ed. Guthrie, 1898, at page 81.

16/35. *compleit* = full, *i. e.* full of weariness and sorrow.

17/7. In the *Clerk's Tale* Chaucer tells the story of patient Grissel, from Boccaccio, *Decameron,* X, 10.

17/19. On patience I must rely perforce.

18. In this poem Scott makes his understanding reproach his wayward affections.

18/14. Chid thyself and no other person.
18/22. To mene [moan] mendis [cures] thee nocht.
18/46. *l. . . . m.* = flounder in the mire.
18/64. "Drynk þat thow hes brewit." When Lord Darnley heard from Sir James Melvil that his fellow-conspirators, Ruthven, Morton, and others, concerned in the murder of Rizzio, had been obliged to flee, he answered, " As they have brewed so let them drink."—*Memoirs of Sir J. Melvil,* Edinburgh, 1735, page 132.

19/22. *on loft,* aloft, *a* is a weakened form of *on.* Cf. *on braid,* abroad, 37/15 ; *on far* = a far, 1/211 ; *on dreich* = adreich, 24/25.

19/36. " *This lady* "—Reason.

20/21. In the *Ballad of Johnnie Armstrang,* who was executed in 1529, is this stanza—

To seek hot water beneath cauld ice
Surely it is great folie ;
I have ask'd grace at a graceless face,
But there is nane for my men and me.

21/22. Made me amorous not of right, *i. e.* not rightly.

21/34. 1882 Edn. reads "trow" instead of "trew." The MS. is indistinct.

21/38. I do not ask for it to be hidden that I'll be careful before loving her again.

22/22. *w. . . w.* = weal or happiness without woe.

23. The version below of this song is from David Herd's *Ancient and Modern Scottish Songs, Heroic Ballads, &c.* Edinburgh, 1776.

This poem was printed by Ramsay in *The Evergreen.* Stanzas 4 and 6 are the same as in Herd, except stanza 4, line 3, Herd has "that" instead of "young." These stanzas are not in the Bannatyne MS.; perhaps they are the work of Allan Ramsay.

The refrain signifies, " For devil a bit from thee will befall her."

1

Return hameward, my heart, again,
And bide where thou wast wont to be,

Thou art a fool to suffer pain,
    For love of ane that loves not thee ;
My heart, let be sick fantasie,
    Love only where thou hast good cause,
Since scorn and liking ne'er agree,
    The fint a crum of thee she fa's.

2

To what effect shou'd thou be thrall?
    Be happy in thine ain free-will
My heart, be never bestial,
    But ken wha does thee good or ill,
And hame with me then tarry still,
    And see wha can best play their,
And let the filly fling her fill, paws
    For fint a crum of thee she fa's.

3

Tho' she be fair, I will not feinzie
    She's of a kin wi' mony mae :
For why they are a felon menzie
    That seemeth good, and are not sae.
My heart take neither sturt or wae ;
    For Meg, for Marjory, or Mause ;
But be thou blyth, and let her gae,
    For fint a crum of thee she fa's.

4

Remember how that Medea
    Wild for a sight of Jason yied ;
Remember how young Cressida
    Left Troilus for Diomede ;
Remember Helen, as we read,
    Brought Troy from bliss unto bare wa's ;
Then let her gae where she may speed,
    For fint a crum of thee she fa's.

5

Because she said, I took it ill
    For her depart my heart was fair,
But was beguil'd ; gae where she will,
    Beshrew the heart that first takes care,
But be thou merry, late and air,
    This is the final end and clause,
And let her feed and fooly fare,
    For fint a crum of thee she fa's.

6

Ne'er dunt again within my breast,
    Ne'er let her slights thy courage spill,
Nor gie a sob, although she sneest,
    She's fairest paid that gets her will.
She geeks as gif I meant her ill,
    When she glaiks paughty in her braws ;
Now let her snirt and fyke her fill
    For fint a crum of thee she fa's.

23/6. *mak* = give.
23/8. *of*, from, *scho fawis* = she gets.

23/18. She is one of a numerous class.
23/19. *fellone menzie* = a bad lot or company.
23/25. *tuik in all* = ill (badly) took [me] in.
24/2. Eagerly resolved to compose this writing: *this present*, these presents, a legal phrase.
24/17. *corss & rent*, body and fortune.
24/19. If she wish to be off I shall go hence.
24/25. *on* dreich = *a* dreich, to a distance ; *on* beich = *a* beich, aloof.
24/32. *kend*, ken it, know it.
24/33. If she pleases to pity me I shall follow her in every season and render her the service of a subject or lover.
25. The editor of the 1882 edition prints this poem in his appendix, and suggests that it is likely to be the work of Scott. Its place in the MS. among a number of poems ascribed by Bannatyne to Scott, as well as the style warrants this supposition.
25/25. *And* = *if: magyn*, this word appears to mean consume.
25/27. The meaning is obscure: *sallis* is indistinct in MS., it might be read sawis. I read *sallis* = chambers: *seilis* perhaps same as *sil*, pl. sillis = faggots. Cf. Jameson's *Scot. Dict.* under *sil*. The meaning would be, " though my chambers are cold (without firewood) yet I'll learn her to be content."
27/1. *þat law* = the law of Cupid. See 29/7.
27/6. And food and sleep do without.
27/35. *I . . . f.* = it should be avoided.
27/36. There were visitations of the plague in Edinburgh in 1529 and 1568 ; the Bannatyne MS. was written during the plague of 1568. Perhaps this poem was written about 1529, the time of the earlier visitation in the sixteenth century.
28/8. *w. d.* = without the victim's will.
28/13, 14. To love and be prudent, To be wanton with caution : and see line 18, where this is said to be impossible.
28/16. *As* not *is the dyiss*. See 20/30, where the same image is used.
29/29. And you have regard to them who care not three straws if they are ignored by you.
29/35. *ago* = agone, escaped.
30/26. Always assert they are chaste.
31/9. Youth and obstinacy are so allied.
31/20. *m. . . . s.* = injure themselves.
31/39, 40. Women hold such men as cannot refrain from them to be worthless.
31/46. Woman is born to breed and feed the fruit of man, *i. e.* children.
32/17. *p. s.* = use signs : because you do not commit yourself, as when you use language.
32/26. Do not stay away on account of rain, *i. e.* of a shower—of trifles.
32/39. " by the wy that all the warld wrocht," an oath.
32/45. Flatter with *fissen*, pith, ability. Earlier editors following Laing read *fyiftene*, which makes nonsense of the line.
33/22. When the figure shows you are pregnant.
33/28. By them who choose to give her geir, *i. e.* something valuable.
33/38. [Who] act so as to injure their husbands' reputation.
33/75. Some cannot keep from lansing (probing) her, etc.
33/95. Much less the larger-hipped, *i. e.* the stronger.
33/101. "to breif ballatis." This phrase is used by Dunbar, " Quhen I wald blythlie ballatis breif " : *To the King*.
34/32. They want to be moaned over, though they moan over no one.

34/34. They want their own way, who rarely know what is right.

34/39, 40. They would be named as the companions of noblemen, though secretly they lean towards lower classes of persons.

34/44. *and* = while: *blekit* = are blacked, are besmutted.

34/62. To avoid having "rewaird" as the end word of both lines, 62 and 64, Hailes substituted "regard" for "rewaird" in this line.

35/22. Let these men go away and cease to believe in their false words.

36. This is a companion to 33, and is "Ane ballat maid to þe derisioun and scorne of wantoun men," as the other is against wanton women. The first two stanzas are similar in both ballads. The version from the Maitland MS., preserved in the library of Magdalene College, Cambridge, is here printed for the first time.

The latter portion of the Bannatyne transcript has been much altered. It contains several difficult lines; the most obscure stanza (lines 113—120) is not in the Maitland transcript.

36/24. *ago* = agone, departed.

36/25. The most sensible anywhere.

36/94. *w. w.* = bankrupt person: perhaps *w. w. r.* = spendthrifts, who have expended their all in debauchery.

36/113. This verse undoubtedly refers to the stories of the reformers about the corruptions of the Roman clergy, and to the satires on the priests which were current at the time of Scott.

Roger Ascham, in his *Schoolmaster*, writes thus: "Time was when Italy and Rome have been, to the great good of us who now live, the best breeders and bringers up of the worthiest men not only for wise speaking, but also for well-doing in all civil affairs that ever was in the world. But now that time is gone; and though the place remain, yet the old and present manners do differ as far as black and white, as virtue and vice. Virtue once made that country mistress over all the world; vice now maketh that country slave to them that before were glad to serve it. All man [mankind] seeth it; they themselves confess it, namely such as be best and wisest amongst them. For sin, by lust and vanity, hath and doth breed up everywhere common contempt of God's word, private contention in many families, open factions in every city, and so making themselves bond to vanity and vice at home, they are content to bear the yoke of serving strangers abroad. Italy now is not Italy as it was wont to be; and therefore now not so fit a place as some do count it for young men to fetch either wisdom or honesty from thence. For surely they will make others but bad scholars that be so ill masters to themselves."

36/114. "saif ane" woman "hecht Pasifie." Apollodorus (III, 1) and Ovid (Met. VIII.) relate the legend of Pasiphae. Her husband Minos wanted to become the ruler of Crete. He declared the country had been given to him by the gods, and to prove his claim asserted that his prayers were always answered. He offered sacrifice to Poseidon, and prayed that a bull might come out of the sea. Poseidon granted the prayer, and sent a bull of great beauty. Minos was so delighted with it that he broke his pledge and sacrificed another bull. His breach of faith raised the ire of the god, and in revenge Poseidon rendered the bull furious, and excited an unholy passion in the breast of Pasiphae. She called Daedalus to her assistance, who made her a figure of wood in the shape of a cow, and covered it with the hide of a cow, and mounted it on wheels. It was then dragged to the pasture ground of the bull; Pasiphae concealed herself in the interior. She became the mother of the Minotaur—the bull-headed monster. Cf. Virgil, En. 6. 14; Cic. De Nat. Deor. III. 19.

The Protestant divines denounced the manners of their time with great

94   *Notes and Illustrations.*

vehemence. The extract, which is quoted at p. ix of the Introduction to this edition, from Knóx's *History* is an interesting commentary on these verses.

36/143. *natouris* = characters.
36/151. Or beware you have not to say: "Woe is me!"
37/15. *on broad* = abroad.
37/22. *the trust* = the true people.

The following poem is given as Scott's by Sibbald. In the Bannatyne MS. it is anon. Sibbald prints "Quod Scott" at the end; but that is not in the MS. now, nor does it appear to ever have been there.

[leaf 218, p. 495.] The well of vertew, and flour of womanheid,
    And patrone vnto patiens;
    Lady of lawty, bayth in word and deid,
    Rycht sobir, sweit, full meik of eloquens,
    Bayth gud and fair; to ȝour magnificens
    I me commend, as I haif done befoir,
    My sempill hairt for now and evir moir.

[leaf 218 b, p. 496] For evir moir I sall ȝow scherwice mak,
    Syne, of befoir, into my mynd I maid;
    Sen first I knew ȝour ladischip, but lak
    Bewty, ȝowth of womanheid ȝe had,
    Withouttin rest my heart cowth nocht evad.
    Thus am I ȝouris and evir sen syne hes bene
    Commandit be ȝour gudly twa fair ene.

    ȝour twa fair ene makis me oft syiss to sing,
    ȝour twa fair ene makis me to syche also,
    ȝour twa fair ene makis me grit conforting,
    ȝour twa fair ene is wycht of all my wo,
    ȝour twa fair ene may no man keip þame fro,
    Withouttin rest that gettis a sycht of þame;
    This of all vertew were ȝe now þe name

    ȝe beir þe name of gentilnes of blud,
    ȝe beir þe name þat mony for ȝow deis,
    ȝe beir þe name ȝe ar bayth fair and gud,
    ȝe beir þe name þat faris þan ȝow seis;
    ȝe beir þe name fortoun and ȝe aggreis,
    ȝe beir þe name of landis of lenth and breid,
    The well of vertew and flour of womanheid.

GLOSSARY.

(*The figures before the | refer to the number of the poem ; the figures after the | to the line of the poem.*)

A

abill, 14/55, likely
abilʒementis, 32/20, dress
abitis, 1/91, obits, offices for the dead
abone, 7/12, above
abuse, *v.* 32/25, reproach
address, *v.* 8/11, prepare
adwersare, 22/3, adversary
affane, *v.* 10/1, attempt. A.S. *fandian*
aganis, 1/8, against
ageit, 36/83 M., aged
ago, *v.* 29/35, 31/16, 36/24, gone
aige, 1/35, age
aikkis, 2/7, oaks
ailis, *v.* 15/1, troubles
aipis, 36/32, apes : here applied to wanton girls
air, 5/12, ? jot. Ice. *aar*
air, 7/19, 23/29, 37/25, early
aith, 36/69 ; aythe, 36/69 M., oath
albeid, 9/7, albeit
alhaill, 9/18, wholly
allegeand, *v.* 31/26, alleging
als, 2/17, 24/20, as
alswa, 11/29, also
amene, 3/1, pleasant. L. *amœnus*
and, 15/31, 32/50, if
ane, 1/184, a
ane, 36/60, on, 36/60 M., one
aneuch, 1/55, enough
anis, 32/48, once
anix, *v.* 38/52, join, bind
annis, 36/107 ; anis, 36/107 M., ass
anschir, 7/3, 11/32, answer
antetewme, 1/145, antiphon ; chant
antiphratis, 34/70, antiphrases : the use of words in an opposite sense to their meaning
a per se, 9/20, first ; incomparable ; like A, the first letter of the alphabet
apill, 36/128, apple
appardoun, *v.* 36/145, pardon
appeill, *v.* 11/33, call
applaud to, *v.* 1/27 ; applawddis, 36/82, commend
apply, *v.* 27/27, 30/44, yield, hearken
ar, *v.* 36/70, are
areir, 1/14, behind. Fr. *arrière*
argun, *v.* 1/54, argue
armipotent, 2/5, potent in arms
aryfe, *v.* 1/187, arrive
asselʒie, *v.* 32/47, assail
at, 34/20, from
athamant, 12/10, diamond, adamant
attingent, *v.* 1/35, attained
attour, 36/62 ; attoure, 36/62 M., over, beyond
auld, 1/145 ; aulde, 36/83 M., old
availʒeis, *v.* 1/109 ; avelʒie, 32/42, avails
avniris, 2/160 ; awer, 36/110 ; aver, 36/110 M., horses ; cf. O.F. *aveir*
avart, *v.* 38/37, avert
aventeur, 13/29, risk
aw, 19/33, awe ; aw, 9/9, [in] awe
awcht, *v.* 33/31, owns
aweryce, 36/98, avarice
awin, 13/12, 29/28, 36/38, 108, own
awysit, *v.* 21/39, advised

B

bab, 13/23, babe
bad, *v.* 18/43, bade, ordered
baggis, 36/91, money bags, property
baikin, *v.* 2/98, *pp.* of baik, to bake
bailfull, 14/5, sorrowful
baill, 2/166, 6/3 ; baillis, 11/23, bale, torment

Glossary.

bairis, 3/53, the game of bars
baith, 15/23; bayth, 1/54; boithe, 36/36 M., both
bakbytand, v. 1/124, backbiting
ban, v. 2/89, curse. Ice. *banna*
band, v. 2/95, bound
bane, 33/38, destruction
banes, 1/83, bones
bar, v. 1/211, to abstain
bargan, 2/104, fight. O.F. *bargaine*
barlabreikis, 3/54, a country game
barrat, 12/12, barrat stone = ? a common causeway stone
barrone, 1/164; barrownis, 1/66, baron
barrowis, 1/183, lists, barriers. O.Fr. *barres*
bassir, 5/6, lower, humbler
bawis, 3/10, balls
be, 2/148, 36/4, by
bed, v. 2/166, bore, endured. A.S. *bidan*
beforrow, 36/40, before
begin, v. 1/19, pray
behufe, sb. 9/25, 10/19, 14/19, command
behuffis, v. 11/19, compels
beich, 24/27. See on beich
beill, 1/6, bell; "to bear the bell" signifies to take the lead
beir, 3/31, beer
beistly, adj. 33/12, animal
beit, v. 11/23, abate
beitis, v. 14/48, beats
bek, v. 1/83, to make obeisance
belangit, v. 1/77, belonged
belappit, v. 8/17; belappis, v. 36/121, enwrapped
beleif, v. 1/205, believe, hope
belyffe, adv. 1/185, immediately
belling, 36/72, rutting; belling tyme = pairing season
bend, v. 24/28, to yoke
bene, 3/2, 8/36, 5/29, 12/1, 20, 22/2; beis, 10/31; bie, v. 33/97, is, are
berne, 1/194, 2/166, youth
besekand, v. 1/47, beseeching
betawcht, v. 33/28, give. A.S. *betaecan*.
bett, v. 2/25, beaten
betuix, 1/44, between
bewche, 2/159; bwche, 2/143, leg. A.S. *boh*
bewis, sb. 4/11, boughs (same etymology as *bewche*)

biblistis, 1/123, ? Bible readers
bich, 36/105; bitche, 36/105 M., bitch
bid, v. 21/38, must
bill, 1/210, writing
billeis, 3/53, comrades, lovers
bind, 37/18, bond; society
birkin bobbynis, 3/18, a knot of birch leaves. *A. Ramsay's Glossary to Evergreen*. Country people used to place them about their houses on account of their fragrance.
birneist, v. 5/29, burnished
birth, 4/11, kind, breed
bismeir, 36/91, whore. A.S. *bismeir*
bissie, 1/43, busy
blaid, 37/13, blade, leaf
blaidis, sb. 36/87 M., blows
blaiknit, 19/4, pale, wan. A.S. *blaecan*
blait, 1/86, timid
blande, v. 1/66; blandit, 11/9, blend
blawdis, 36/87, blows
ble, 19/4, complexion. A.S. *bléo*
bleir, v. 1/86, blind, blur
blek, v. 36/140; blekit, 34/44, stain
blenche ferme, 13/8: In Blanche holding a vassal makes a small payment in lieu of all services to the superior.
blenk, sb. 15/26, glance
blenkyne, v. sb. 18/41, blinking
blin, v. 2/104, desist. A.S. *blinnan*
blude, 1/66, blood
blunder, sb. 2/149, confusion
bobbynis, 3/18, knots of leaves. Cf. Gaelic *baban*
bodeis, 1/86, persons
boir, 17/3, pore of the skin
boith, 37/8, both
boitis, 12/20, boats
bot, 1/123, 212, 9/16; but, 1/114; butt, 36/27 M., without, except; 29/25, only
boun, adj. 2/91, ready
boun, v. 33/84, to prepare. Cf. Icel. verb *bua*, to prepare, pp. *buinn*
bound, v. 29/25, fettered
boutting, 36/88 M.; bowtyne cleth, 36/88, a thin cloth, boulting cloth (O.Fr. *buleter*): venus bowtyne cleth: cestus of Venus
bowgill, 2/172, bugle
bowis, 3/18, boughs. See bewis

Glossary. 97

bowrdis, 1/211, jests. O.Fr. *bourde*
bra, 2/145 ; brae, face of a hill
brace, *v.* 1/215; braice, 33/44 ; brasing, 33/53 ; braisit, 13/6 ; embrace
braid, *v.* 2/145, started, rushed. A.S. *braedan*
braid, on, 37/15, abroad
brand, 2/165, sword
brane, 33/102, brain
breif, *v.* 33/101, write. L. *breve*
breir, 1/206 ; breiris, 2/17, brier
brek, *v.* 33/102, break
breþir, *sb.* 27/41, brothers
bricht, 5/29, 12/2, bright
brodding, *v.* 2/16, spurring. A.S. *brord*
broich, 2/40, on broich, on tap
bruke, *v.* 1/194, possess. A.S. *brúcan*
bruckill, 33/33 ; brukle, 31/3, inconstant
brutall, 36/20 ; brutell, 36/20 M., brutal
brute, 37/9, brood, offspring
bucklar, *sb.* 2/165, buckler, shield
buchone, 3/50, ? on buchone wyis = ? to obtain her most cherished favours
buke, 1/108, book
bukkis, *sb.* 36/72, bucks
bukkit, *v.* 2/105, incited, pushed
burd, *v.* 19/29, burned, behoved
burd, 36/70, bird
burge, *v.* 37/11, to bud. Cf. Fr. *bourgeonner*
busk, *sb.* 14/47, bush
but, 1/114 ; butt, 36/27 M., without (*see* bot)
by, *v.* 2/88 ; byand, *v.* 2/115, buy
by, 3/21, against
byd, *v.* 8/8, 16 ; 23/2, abide, remain
bynge, *v.* 1/83, cringe (Icel. *beygia,* to bow)

C

cace, *sb.* 18/35, condition
cachis, *v.* 3/38, hides. Cf. Fr. *cacher*
caice, 32/49, case
cald, 27/19, cold
cast, *v.* 1/33 ; kest, 2/76, throw off ; 32/27, determine
ceiss, *v.* 1/95, stop
celsitude, 1/193, greatness, might
chaipis, *v.* 36/30, escapes
chanteris, 1/127 ? *pl.* of chanter: the chief singer or priest of a chantry

chappit, *v.* 33/67, knocked
charbucle, 1/219, carbuncle
chawcht, 33/29, catch, get
cheir, 1/62, cheer, fare
chene, 9/35, chain
chift, *v.* 33/71, shift, remove
chop, *v.* 1/62, barter
chucking, *v.* 33/50, fondling
clair, 2/52, completely
clais, 3/45, ? hurdles, hedges
clap, *v.* 33/44, 73, stroke, fondle
clattrer, 30/41, tattler, tell tale
clawin, *v.* 33/27, scratched
cleif, 1/34, cleave. A.S. *clifan*
cleive, *v.* 33/47, open. A.S. *cliofan*
clenge, *v.* 38/11 ; clengit, 38/30, acquit (legal term)
clergie, 1/102, learning
clerk, 1/164, clergyman, scholar
clething, 1/178, clothing
clippit, *v.* 34/70, called
clown, *adj.* 3/20, clownish
cluddis, 12/4, clouds
clym, *v.* 33/43, climb
coft, *v.* 13/28, 19/24, 36/102, bought. A.S. *ceapian*
coile, 33/68, coal
coistlie, 1/178, costly
coite, 36/150, literally coats, cover
cokkillis, 3/32, cockles
combure, *v.* 14/5, consume, burn
commamis, 3/32, ? young coal fish : a fish allied to the cod. It gets its name from the pigment on skin, which blackens the hands when these fish are touched.
commend, 11/2, present
communis, 1/150, common people
compleit, *v.* 11/25, 16/35, ended
compt, *v.* 2/132 ; comptis, 36/78 M., count
compt, *v.* 36/118, recount
confidder, *v.* 35/11, confederate, keep company with
confort, 10/8, encouragement
confound, *v.* 34/58, come to ruin
confusit, *adj.* 31/29, confused, absurd
consate, 1/33 ; consaitis, 34/3, concept, thought
consequent, 1/165, in due order
consorss, *sb.* 1/180, association
consorss, *v.* 31/9, joined
constrynd, 36/21, constrained
coppis, 36/124, drinking cups

98   Glossary.

corse, 13/30; corss, 1/178, 24/17, 31/13, body
cossis, v. 13/31, exchange. A.S. ceósan
counter, v. 2/34, encounter
course, 32/5, career
courtas, 34/75, courteous
covettyiss, 34/16, covetousness
cowet, v. 36/127; covettis, 34/43, covet
cowth, 1/143, well known
crab, v. 34/76, become ill-tempered
crabit, 1/148, ill-tempered, provoked
crak, 2/169, explosion; 2/176, talk
creddens, 35/23; creddence, 32/36, credence
crewall, 27/32, cruel
criselleit, 12/9, chrysolite, golden stone
croce, 1/49, cross
cumd, v. 5/16, come
cunnyng, 1/102, skill
cunȝe, 36/90; conȝie, 33/29; cwnȝe, 36/90 M., coin
cuplit, v. 1/180, coupled
cure, 1/34, 6/15, charge, tutelage
cure, v. 9/23; cureis, 29/29; curis, 36, care for
curius, 27/37, abounding in care
curpall, 2/169, crupper
cursit, v. 1/155, excommunicated
cursour, 2/152, 36/110; cursoure, 36/110 M., horse
cur-tyk, 36/105; curr-doig, 36/105 M., a mongrel dog
cuschett, 13/38, ring-dove
cute, 1/109; cutis, 29/29, trifle
cuvatyce, 1/118, greed

D

daifit, v. 1/90, pret. of deave, to deafen
daill, v. 30/3, dally, to have intercourse
daly, 32/22, daily
dang, v. 2/8, past t. of ding, to overcome, knock down
dantoun, v. 1/55, subdue, tame
dapill, 36/126, mixed with gray
dar, v. 5/37, dare
dargeis, 1/90, dirges
dasy, 1/222, daisy
de, v. 9/24, 15/18, die
debait, sb. 2/1, contest
decoir, v. 1/17, 178, decorate

decreitis, v. 36/113, ? decrees, judges, censures
defame, 32/50, ill-fame
defend, v. 32/50, prohibit
degest, 27/13, 33/89, properly adjusted
deid, adj. 1/83, dead
deid, sb. 2/67, 16/7, death
deid, sb. 30/19; deidis, 36/19, deed
deir, adj. 2/39, costly
deir, sb. 3/27, deer
deir, sb. 38/39, harm
denkest, 33/85, sauciest
denner, 2/100; dennaris, 2/80, dinner
denteis, 2/39, dainties
deploir, v. 8/33, deplore
dertis, 7/9, darts
descrywe, v. 1/171, describe
dett, 1/23, duty
devoir, 30/50, duty
dewlie, 1/17, duely
dewtie, 1/129, duty
dewyss, 5/30, device
diamant, 12/8, diamond
dicht, v. 2/80, pp. of dicht, to prepare
discrepance, 1/29, 22/10, discordance
disione, 2/75, breakfast
dispyss, 11/5, wrong
dispyt, v. 34/25, dispise
diseiss, 24/22, 26/24, uneasiness
dissait, 36/135 M., deceit
docht, 5/20, could. A.S. dugan
doggitless, adv. 19/10, unworthily. Cf. A.S. duguth
dollour, 14/33, dolor
done, v. 11/5, do
dout, sb. 36/27, fear
dow, sb. 1/215, dove
dow, v. 33/22; docht, pret. 5/20, to be able
dowbill, 28/21, 36/103; double, 36/103 M.; dowble, 1/222, deceitful
dowbilnes, 1/129, two facedness
dowsy, 2/11, twelve
dowt, v. 31/36, fear
drafe, 2/161, excrement
dre, v. 14/33, 15/3, endure
dreich, 24/25. See on dreich
dress, v. 5/20, 18/7, 20/13, address, redress
drest, 2/80, prepared
drevin, v. 1/129, pp. of drive, to urge strongly
duchty, 2/10, doughty

Glossary.

dulce, 1/222, sweet
dule, 7/23, 15/29, sorrow. Fr. *deuil*
dullit, 14/29, 15/15, torpid, dulled
dyiss, 28/16, dice

E

e, 1/38, 18/41 ; ene, *pl.* 38/15 ; ein, *pl.* 1/86, eye
efeir, 38/35, exactly proportioned to, fitly
effrey, *v.* 5/35, fear
eik, 15/30, also
eikwall, 2/43, just
eindill, *v.* 34/45, to become jealous
eir, 1/38, ear
eiss, 13/13, ease
eit, *v.* 1/74, eat
ellis, 31/24, else
enarmit, *v.* 1/182, armed
endlang, 37/10, along
enforss, *v.* 1/181 ; enforsis, 33/55, oblige, compel
epistollis, 1/113, epistles
erd, 9/20, earth
erdly, 16/44, earthly
eschamit, *v.* 34/74, ashamed
espy, *v.*; espye, *v.* 36/3, see
estait, *sb.* 1/30, condition
ethis, 2/87, oaths
everichone, 3/16, every one
evir-bone, 7/37, ivory
evirilk, 9/36, every
exort, *v.* 10/7, entreat
expart, 22/17, expert, 10/12, experienced
express, *adv.* 5/21, 19/8, expressly

F

facournd, 11/9, 32/11 ; eloquent
faid, 32/30; feid, 2/69, 5/9, 19/8, feud, quarrel, ill-will. M.E. *fede*
faik, *v.* 18/47, grasp. A.S. *facian*
fair, *v.* 27/24 ; fairin, *v.* 2/78 ; fure, 14/1, to go, to fare
fairsing, *v.* 1/123, stuffing
fais, 2/111, 31/36, foes
fallow, *v.* 23/31, follow
falsatt, 3/24 ; falset, 34/10, falsehood
falt, 1/138, 11/13, want
famist, 1/137, famished, starved
famyny, 3/28 ; famenene, 34/69 ; femenene, 14/25, women kind
fan, *v.* 25/28, ? to put up with, to feign contentment
fane, 21/22, fain

fannis, *v.* 36/105 ; faunis, 36/105 M.; fawin, 33/25, to long for. Cf. Icel. *fagna*, to be glad
fary, 25/16, ? confusion, or ? if connected with A.S. *faran*, to go
fastlingis, 3/19, well nigh
fawin, *v.* 33/25. See fannis
fawis, *v.* 3/8, *v.* 23/8, falls, obtains, gets
feale, 1/212, fealty
fecht, *v.* 2/48, fight
feckill, 32/11, fickle
fecound, 38/45, fertile
feid, *v.* 25/26, 31/47, feed
feidit, *v.* 2/164, challenged
feind, 23/8, devil (feind a crum = devil a bit)
feir, 2/96, 5/9, companion
feir, 2/103, 32/45, fright, fear
fek, 36/138, make, effect
fel, *v.* 15/23, fail
fell, 2/4, mettlesome
fellone, 23/19, wicked
felȝie, *v.* 32/45 ; felȝeit, 18/47, fail
fenȝeit, *adj.* 20/29, 21/21, 35/7, false
fenȝeit, *sb.* 7/27, falsehood
fenȝie, *v.* 23/17, feign
fer, 13/28, far
fermit, *v.* 13/4, confirmed
fery, 2/64, active
fey, 2/189, faith
fibilnes, 3/24, feebleness
fillok, 23/15 ; fillokkis, 33/63, young mare, giddy lass
filly, 23/31, fop
firth, 4/14, forest
flaw, 2/176, a sudden burst of passion
fle, 2/125, flight
fle, *v.* 27/35 ; fleis, *v.* 34/38, to flee
fleich, *v.* 36/45 ; fleiche, *v.* 32/45 ; fleische, *v.* 33/13, flatter
fleme, *v.* 38/45 ; flemis, 29/33 ; flemit, 1/130, chace. A.S. *facian*
flesch, 1/74, beef; animal food
fling, *v.* 23/15, dance about
flit, *v.* 27/11, move
flureist, 37/14 ; flurist, *adj.* 1/217, flourishing
fo, 22/16, foe
foche, *v.* 2/96, break away (also written fotch, *Jamieson*)
foirgifanis, 1/161, forgiveness
foirse, *v.* 36/137, foresee
for quhy, 5/29, 7/6, 8/14, 34/7, 71, because

Glossary.

forbeir, 32/53, spare
force, *sb.* 1/26, fortitude
forfair, *v.* 18/23, perish. A.S. *forfaran*
foregane, 38/15, before
forloir, *v.* 6/6; forlorne, 36/66, lost
formois, 1/217, beautiful
forrow, 36/40 M. (= forouch), before
forvey, *v.* 32/15, go astray. O.Fr. *forvoyer*
forʒet, *v.* 27/47, forget
foundis, *v.* 3/39, goes. A.S. *fundian*
foursum, 2/131, four together
fouth, 1/138; fowth, 38/29, plenty, abundance
fow, 2/161, full
fowne, 2/64, fawn
fowness, 2/98, fulness
fowsum, 36/13; fulsum, 36/13 M.; fulsome
fra, 1/36, by
fra, 1/130, through
fra, 2/185, 31/1, 36/21, 54, when
frak, 1/181, bold, vigorous. A.S. *frec*
frane, *v.* 36/45, insist, press. A.S. *fregnan*
fraude, *v.* 36/32 M.; frawd, *v.* 36/32, defraud, cheat
freikis, 2/4, fellows
freir, 1/54, friar
fremmit, 15/6, 32/30, 34/37, unlucky, estranged, strange
fremmitness, 19/7, strangeness, unfriendliness
frennessy, 32/1, frenzy
frigging, 33/62, masturbation
fruitioun, 1/68, power
fule, 23/3; fulis, 36/8; fuilis, 36/8 M., fool
fulgent, 1/217, shining
fuliche, 34/13, foolish
fund, *v.* 30/11, found
funder, *v.* 2/147, founder
furdir, *v.* 29/41, succeed, advance
fure, *v.* 14/1, bear, carry. Icel. *faera*.
furthschaw, *v.* 9/9, forthshew
fute, 1/183, foot
fyisene, 32/45, vigour. Cf. O.F. *foison*
fyld, *v.* 2/160; fyle, 30/25; fylit, 36/31, dirtied, defiled, stained
fyre-fangit, *v. pp.* 1/74, burnt

G

ga, *v.* 2/150. 23/15, 23; gane, 9/36, go; gaiss, 14/30; gais, 24/23; gois, 3/11; gang, 27/12: parts of gae, or ga, to go
gaidis, 36/85 M.; gawdis, 36/85, tricks, games
gaill, *v.* 3/26, to call; golk to gaill, cuckoo to call or sing. A.S. *galan*
gaiss, *v.* 29/24; gess, 1/131, guess
gait, 37/27; gaitis, 2/179, ways
galay, 12/19, galley
gallandis, 3/11, gallants
galʒart, 2/38, pleasure-seeking
gan, *v.* 2/172, began
gap, 33/75, ?
gar, *v.* 1/19, to cause; garris, 5/7; gart, 18/42, 21/27; gartit, 36/55
garth, 8/25, garden
geif, 33/98, give
geir, 1/118, 33/28, 36/96, property of any kind, money
gelly, 2/163, ? jolly. A.S. *gal*
geme, 24/1; gemmis, 1/181, game
genetryce, 1/5, mother
gent, 1/209, 17/8, gentle
gentillis, 14/44, high born persons
gentrice, 33/81, genteel
genʒeild, 34/62, reward
gess, *v. See* gaiss
gettin, 36/96 M.; gottin, *v.* 36/96, obtained
giff, 1/157; giffe, 1/193, if; gif, 31/15, unless
glaik, *v.* 18/42; glak, *v.* 30/33, to look foolish, to fool
glaikis, *sb.* 36/16, dumps
glaikit, *adj.* 26/16, foolish, thoughtless
gloir, 1/19, glory
goif, *v.* 18/42, to look foolish, stare. Cf. Germ. *gaffen*.
golk, 3/26, cuckoo. Is. *gouk-r*
goun, 14/44, 33/82, gown
govirnance, 32/24, government
gowlis, 12/15, marigolds
graif, *adj.* 32/43, grave
graif, *sb.* 6/4, ? grasp
grane, *v.* 36/46, groan
graping, *v.* 33/53, groping
graue, *v.* 15/20, gravit, *v.* 1/117, to impress deeply, engraved
gravit, *adj.* 7/36, carved
gre, 38/68, recompense
grediar, 1/131; grydiar, 33/90, greedier
greitis, *v.* 36/67, greets, weeps

Glossary.

greting, v. 1/224, praying
grit, 1/50, 224, great; grittest, 1/131, 33/87, greatest
growme, 2/118; grumis, 3/15, man
grufling, v. 38/3, grovelling
grunche, v. 36/92, grumble
grunching, sb. 29/14, grumbling
grund, 2/147, ground
grunʒe, 36/92, face, mouth. Fr. *groin*
gucking, sb. 33/52, trifling, fooling
gudeman, 1/192; guidman, 1/184, husband
gudly heid, 17/15, beauty
guid, 1/32, good
gwerdoun, 34/62, reward
gyd, 19/36, guide
gyiss, 2/49, 33/77, fashion, bearing
gymmer, 3/14, sprucer, neater
gymp, 33/77, delicately

H

haell, 1/212, health
haif, v. 1/51, 5/22, 37/9, have
haill, 34/5, whole
hairis, 3/38, hares
halkis, v. 3/37, fish with hawks
hals, 21/23; halss, 33/43, neck
haltand, 25/17, haughty
halye, 1/51, holy
hame, 1/title, home
hamewart, 23/1, homeward
hane, v. 33/94, spare. O.Icel. *hegna*
hankis, v. 36/4 M., fastens
hant, v. 36/84, 33/3, haunt, practice. Fr. *hanter*
hap, 2/50, chance
harbary, v. 1/205, bring to harbour
hareit, v. 1/140, harried
harmisay, 30/41, alas
hart, 13/7; hairt, 13/1, 38/43, heart
hartit, 36/52 M.; hairtit, 36/52, hearted
haviness, 7/24, heaviness
havingis, 30/26, 34/4, behaviour
he, 11/35, 19/18, 25/17; hie, 1/18, high
hecht, v. 32/34, pt. t. of hate, to promise. A.S. *hátan*
hecht, sb. 36/69, promise
hecht, v. 36/114, named. A.S. *hátan*
heich, 24/25, 38/6, high
heid, 36/4, head
heidismen, 1/141, headmen, masters
heir, 38/33, hearing

heit, 31/14, heat
helsum, 13/1, full of life
hes, v. 1/55, 68, 213, 5/11, 31/14, 37/5; hess, 29/39; he[s], 22/13, hast, has, have
hett, 2/23, 20/21, hot
hewche, 2/157; huche, 2/141, steep hill
hiemaill, 12/18, wintry. L. *hiemalis*
hienes, 1/159, highness
hippit, 33/95, hipped
hird, v. 13/21, guard
hittin, v. 2/33, hit
ho, 22/15, halt
hoile, 33/3, hole
hoip, 1/9; howp, 13/3, hope
horss, to, v. 3/58, to assist to mount
howbeid, 20/5, 32/25, howbeit
huke, 36/3, hook
hully, 3/70, moderately
hurdeis, 33/94, hips
hurdome, 36/123, whoredom
husbandis, 1/174, husbandmen
hyne, 14/39, 24/19, hence

I

idolatheit, 1/153, idolatrous
ilk, 7/9, 34/44, each
illustrat, 1/1, illustrious
imbassatis, 1/185, ambassadors
in, 9/34, into
inarmit, v. 24/4, embraced
incertane, 28/16, uncertain
inclusit, v. 31/27, inclosed, controlled
inglis, 5/40, English
ingraif, v. 1/214, engrave
ingyne, sb. 1/98, genius, capacity. L. *ingenium*
inleid, v. 17/13, continue
inorme, 36/139, vicious
inteir, 27/43, entirely
intill, 1/210, in
inwart, 7/42, 8/39, 9/2, within, inward
I wiss, 9/21, 14/38, certainly. A.S. *ge-wiss*

J

jak, 2/163, a short coat of mail, or perhaps of leather
japit, v. 33/79, debauched
jasp, 12/9, jasper
jassink, 12/9, jacinth
jeigis, 33/58, jigs, tunes
jo, 22/13, joy. Fr. *joie*

jott, v. 33/81, to strut about
just, v. 2/71, joust
iusting, sb. 2/title, jousting

K

keilis, v. 12/5; keild, 2/26, 2/156, 17/23, to kill
keir, v. 1/150, to drive away
ken, v. 35/5; kennis, 19/29, to know
ken, v. 38/55, direct, guide
ken, sb. 37/28, view
kendillit, v. 28/8, kindled
kest, v. 2/76. See cast
kin, 1/84; kynd, 36/108, kindred
kin, 18/19, kind, species
kirk, 1/21, church
kirkmen, 1/44, churchmen
kis, v. 1/127, ?
kittie, 34/19, usually giddy or wanton woman, here an *adj.* = wanton
knaw, v. 37/8, know
knittin, v. 2/31, knit
kocatrice, 12/5, basilisk. A fabulous serpent hatched from a cock's egg, who could kill by merely breathing or looking at a person.
koy, 32/54, concealed
kuikis, 1/127, ? excrement; cf. Icel. *kuka*
kune, v. 31/6, know, appreciate. A.S. *cunnian*
kynd, 17/37, nature; 32/4, manner
kyndnes, 2/95, friendship

L

laice, 33/42, lace
laich, 3/45, low
laidis, 36/84 M., lads
laif, 7/12, 8/26; lave, 38/79, remainder
laik, 11/16, lack, want
laill, 3/29; leill, 1/139, 36/66 M.; leilest, 5/24, faithful
lair, 5/25, 18/18, 22/1, lore
lair, v. 18/46, to bemire, to flounder in the mire
lairdis, 1/147, landlords, nobles, lords
laist, 10/26, last
lait, 7/19, 23/29, late
laith, 36/86; laythe, 36/86 M., loath
laittandly, 34/40, hiddenly
laittis, 36/84; leittis M., 36/84, behaviour, manners
lakit, v. 36/133 M.; lakkit, v. 36/133, scolded, reproached

lanciss, 2/62, lances
landmen, 1/156, land-owners
lane, v. 21/38, 33/22, hide, conceal
lang, 8/9, 33/61, long
langsum, 19/30, tedious
lansing, 33/76, ? probing
lapstaris, 3/33, lobsters
lasar, 13/34, leisure
lassis, 1/53, girls
lat, v. 21/35, 30/50; latt, 23/23, 33/42; lattis, 19/37; lett, 20/20; lute, 1/81, 21/19, to let, to allow
lathly, 27/44, loathsome
lauboure, v. 1/15, to labour
lauchfullie, 36/58 M.; lawchtfully, 36/58, lawfully
lawar, 34/40, lower
lawch, v. 34/25; lawchis, 36/68; lewche, *pret.* 2/137, laugh
lawchter, 33/26, brood
lawchtter, 2/170, laughter
lawdis, 1/53, 36/84, laddies, boys
lawtie, 1/100; lawty, 14/16, loyalty, fidelity
le, v. 10/23, lie
le, 22/21; lie, 2/119, security, shelter
leale, 1/212, loyalty
leddy, 5/17, lady
leid, v. 27/44, 36/2, lead
leid, 5/25, 34/7, person. A.S. *leod*
leif, v. 1/46, 62, 8/6, live
leif, v. 19/1, 36/86; leife, 36/6, leave
leif, sb. 37/13, leaf
leifing, sb. 1/147, living
leifsum, 36/57 M.; lesum, 36/57, allowable
leik, 2/132, leek
leill, 1/139, 34/28, faithful
leindis, v. 34/40, leans, inclines. (*Hailes, Glossary to Ancient Scottish Poems.*)
leir, *adv.* 33/79; lever, *adv.* 8/3, rather
leir, v. 1/78, teach
leis, sb. 1/92, 29/19, lies
leist, 8/23, least
leit, v. 34/7, permit, tolerate
leive, 21/1, to get clear of, to leave
lelalie, 1/100, faithfully
lempettis, 3/33, limpets
len, v. 1/204, lend, give
lest, v. 1/15, 36/58, last, continue
lesum, 36/57, lawful
lett, v. 20/20, to cause to stop
letterit, 1/52, lettered

Glossary. 103

leud, 1/156, common, worthless
lever, 8/3, rather
liberos, 1/204, children
lichorie, 36/121 M., lechery
licht, 32/13, merry
lichtly, v. 34/43; lychtleis, 29/21; lychtleis, 5/12; to contemn
lickly, 34/45, gladly, likely
lidder, 2/62, late. Cf. A.S. *lith*
lie, 2/119, shelter, peace
lippin, v. 19/40, trust
list, v. 21/45, 33/28, 38/63, it pleases
lo, 1/53, low, humble
loche, 2/98, a kind of fish, loach, groundling: it used to be caught in the Water of Leith. *Grant's Old and New Edinburgh.*
loft, 36/104, above
loif, 35/18, praise. A.S. *lof*
lot, 1/218, lily
loun, 2/97, 33/87, boy, rogue
lovingis, 38/36, 62, praises
lowp, v. 13/1, jump
lowse, v. 38/61; lowis, 33/42, loosen
luchrie, 1/77, lechery
lufe, *sb.* 1/110; lufe, 1/42, 218; luif, *sb.* 36/7 M.; luife, *sb.* 36/122 M., loif, 38/81; love
luffarris, 36/1, lovers
lufly, 17/33, lovely
luik, *sb.* 21/25, look
luke, v. 33/1, look
luknyt, v. 9/35, locked
lusty, 11/15, lustiest, 12/21, pleasant, beautiful
luvar, 9/17, lover
luvis, v. 35/6, loves
lyking, 5/17; lykingis, 34/26, favourite
lymmer, *adj.* 1/53, impudent
lyne, 1/100, line
lyone, 1/2, lion
lyth, 2/122, joint. A.S. *lith*
lyttit, 1/156, ? smeared

M

ma, v. 11/23, may
ma, v. 11/32; maik, 24/9; maikis, 23/28; mak, 23/26, make
ma, 23/18, more in number
magyn, v. 25/25, ? consume
maik, *sb.* 1/198, match. A.S. *maca*
mailis, 25/25, rents. A.S. *mæl*
mair, 35/24, more; maist, 1/7, 32/42, most

maiss, v. 14/31; meiss, v. 30/20, 33/60, 36/148, comfort, please, calm
maistrice, 5/8, mastery
malignis, v. 27/34; maling, 30/17, maligns
mallure, 14/3, misery. Fr. *malheur*
man, *aux.* v. 18/63, must
mane, 23/28, 32/42; mene, v. 10/2, 18/22; menit, 34/32; menis, 34/32, bemoan
mangit, v. 1/79, wasted
mankit, page 1, line 7, imperfect. Fr. *manquer*
manrent, 29/13, homage
mantand, v. 1/92, mumbling
mareit, v. 1/73, married
margareit, 12/11, pearl
marrowis, 3/42, partners
maveis, 3/7, blackbird
may, 2/181, maid
meine, v. 1/82, mean
meir, 1/142, 36/109, mare
meittand, v. 13/33, exhausting; *pr. p.* of mate or mait, to weary out
mell, v. 1/97, meddle. O.Fr. *mesler*
mends, v. 18/22, amends
mene, v. 10/2; menis, 34/32; menit, 34/32, moan
menʒe, 1/79; menʒie, 23/19, company. O.Fr. *maignee*
mensworne, 36/69, perjured
merciall, 31/35, 34/55, martial
mess, 1/97, the mass
midhill, 2/148, half way
miscareit, v. 1/75, injured
mishaif, v. 32/49, misbehave
misken, v. 34/15, disown
misknawin, v. 29/30, ignored
miss, 1/75, 38/18, fault
mo, 10/25; moir, 32/2, 33/89, more
moif, v. 27/3, 36/97, mvfe, 31/18, move
mok, 2/127, mock
mokkis, v. 36/68 M., mocks
mone, 2/73, moon
monebrunt, 33/65, moonstruck
moneth, 3/1, month
mony, 35/5; monye, 1/92; moniest, 32/40, many, most
mort-mvmlingis, 1/92, prayers for the dead
mot, v. 36/142, may
mound, 38/42, pure. L. *mundus*
mull, 36/107; mwle, 36/107 M., mule
muttoun, 31/32, sheep

mycht, *v.* 2/98, might, was able
myn3onis, 3/57, servants, favourites

N

na, 1/59, no
neir, 1/22, near
nemmit, *v.* 34/39, named
nicht, 32/15, 33/66, night
no, 37/17
nocht, 1/57, 33/94, 36/151, not
nochtis, *sb. pl.* 37/17, reprobate
nolt, *v.* 38/71, will not
non, 32/18, none
none, 2/79, noon
nor, 11/22, than
nottis, *sb.* 4/12, notes
nowdir, 23/21 ; nowþir, 21/3, neither
noyand, *v.* 1/124, *pres. p.* of noy, to annoy, to injure
nuke, 33/3 ; nwikis, *pl.* 1/124, nook
nureiss, *v.* 13/22 ; nvreist, 34/57, nourish
nyce, *adj.* 20/8, 36/101 ; nyiss, 25/23 ; nycest, *sup.* 33/91, fastidious
nychtbouris, 1/124, neighbours
nynnis, 33/92, ? nonce, opportunity
nynte, 1/197, ninth

O

occupyis, *v.* 3/12, employs
ocht, 11/6, 31/24, any thing
of, 1/105 ; off, 1/134, 36/88 M., from
offerand, *sb.* 38/66, offering
on, 13/22, in, during
on beich = abeich, *adv.* 24/27, aloof
on dreich = adreich, *adv.* 24/25, at a distance
onhapp, 36/123 M., unlucky
ony, 1/51, any
opin, 33/74 ; oppin, 1/49, open
or, 2/79, before
ordand, *v.* 31/45, ordained
ouir, 1/147 ; our, 5/8 ; oure, 3/25 ; our, 2/128, over, to
ourset, *v.* 20/18, upset
ourslyd, *v.* 19/41, slide
oursylis, *v.* 32/40, beguiles
ourtane, *v.* 2/173, overtaken
ourthraw, 19/31, overthrow
ourweill, *v.* 3/22, wells over, overflows
out-throwcht, 12/7 ; owt-throwch, 3/38 ; outthrow, 7/10, through out
owklie, 1/91, weekly
oxsteris, 13/31, arms. A.S. *Oxtan*

P

paip, 1/67, pope
paiparis, 1/82, papers
pairty, 1/198, equal
pal3ardy, 36/82 ; pal3ardrie, 36/82 M., whoredom. Fr. *paillard*
paly, 12/3, pale
pane, 32/46 ; panis, 1/50, pain
pang, 2/161, crammed
parramowris, *adv.* 32/46, like paramours
pastance, 36/15, pastime
pastouris, 1/57, pastors
pawis, 23/14, parts, or steps, ? from Fr. *pas*
peax, 1/10 ; peice, 32/51, peace
pentioun, 1/73, pension: allowances in kind, such as oatmeal and malt
pepill, 1/115, people
perforss, 17/19, of necessity
perfyte, 15/31, perfect, complete
perigall, 8/21, equal. Fr. *par égal*
perqueir, 1/46, decently, conscienceously
persit, *v.* 11/17, pierced
personis, 1/132, parsons
pert, 32/17, expert
perverst, 36/81 M.; perwersit, 36/81, perverted
petefull, 38/60, pityful
petie, 32/7, pity
petously, 32/28, piteously
peirles, 13/19, peerless, without peer
pilleis, 3/55, pillars
pischt, *v.* 2/79, pissed
pissans, 14/15, puissance
plaid, *v.* 3/13, played
plaig, 27/36, plague
plane, 10/1, 21/10, 30/37, 33/78, open, openly ; 27/26, full
planeist, *v.* 34/9, plenished
play, *v.* 2/183, 33/70, fornicate
plene, *v.* 13/37, complain
plesance, 6/12, pleasure
plesand, *adj.* 1/7 ; plesander, 12/20, pleasant
plet, *v.* 26/8, folded
plicht, *v.* 2/68, 11/40, plighted, placed. A.S. *plihtan*
plucking, *v.* 33/53, pulling
policie, 1/45, government
port, 10/6, deportment
powin, 2/68, peacock. Fr. *paon*
poyettis, 36/113, poets
practik, 32/50 ; practikis, 36/47 M.;

Glossary. 105

prectikis, 36/47, practice, art. Cf. Fr. *practique*
preche, *v.* 36/45; preiche, *v.* 36/45, preach
prefulgent, 12/2, shining
preif, *v.* 17/35, 36/125 M., try
preiss, *v.* 5/37, 32/14; prees, 36/37, press
preiss, *v.* 32/21; preysis, *v.* 5/1; prysit, *pp.* 31/44, value
prelettes, 1/46, prelates
prent, *v.* 1/209, print
prescryvis, *v.* 1/58, condemns
preservand, *v.* 1/36, preserving
presome, *v.* 5/33, presume
prevy, 32/17, secret
prikkis, *sb.* 3/44, the points in the centre of the butts
proif, *v.* 38/84; prufe, 10/17; pruffit, 20/33, prove
promit, *v.* 35/13, promise
proper, 9/28, goodly
prophane, 36/47 M., unholy
proppis, 36/125, ? objects
propyne, 14/18, gift, good will offering
protestandis, 1/145, protestants
prounʒe, *v.* 36/95; prwnʒe, *v.* 36/95 M., adorn
prow, 1/215, profit, honour
pruffit, *v.* 20/33, proved
pryd, *sb.* 38/59, pride
prye, *v.* 36/125, try
pund, *v.* 1/150, poind, empound
pur, 5/10; pure, 1/39, 150, 36/48, poor
pursevandis, 1/149, officers who attend on heralds. Six were in attendance on the Lyon King at arms
pynd, *v.* 2/84, 11/42, 36/18; pynit, 17/2, pained, tortured
pyne, *v.* 24/16, suffer

Q

quaver-caice, 33/47, quiver-case, female pudenda
quenry, 36/124, loose women
quent, 1/143, 34/3, familiar, known
quba, 1/74, 11/23, who
quhair, 1/132, where
quhairfoir, 6/19, wherefore
quhais, 9/21, 33/31; quhois, 37/13, whose
quhat, 1/75, 34/2, what

quhattane, 26/16, what kind of
quhay, 3/32, whey
quhen, 36/67; quhone, 36/67 M., when
quhiddir, 27/9, whether
quhilk, 1/12, 6/4; quhilkis, *pl.* 1/211, who
quhill, 36/64, 2/16, 10/24; quhyll, 36/46 M., until
quhip, *v.* 33/93, take it nimbly
quhome, 7/17; quhom, 11/4, whom
quhy, 27/25, why; the quhy, the reason
quhyle, 27/19; quhylss, 36/112; quhylis, 36/112 M., sometimes
quhyt, 33/83; quhyte, 8/25; quhyttar, 38/31, white
quhytliest, 33/93, most delicate looking
quyt, *v.* 34/75, acquit
quytclame, *v.* 24/31, 34/76, resign, renounce

R

ra, 2/140, roe
rachis, 3/40, hounds
raid, *v.* 2/168, rode
raifand, *v.* 1/125, tearing
raik, *v.* 18/45; raikit, 2/74, go, wander
raiss, *v.* 2/100, arose
raith, *v.* 9/11, anger
rakles, *adj.* 33/2, reckless; reklesly, *adv.* 31/54
rame, *v.* 36/51, roar. A.S. *hréman*
rane, *sb.* 32/26, rain
rank, *adj.* 32/44, firm; rankest, 1/188, greatest rank
rathest, *adj.* 32/35, quickest
rebute, *v.* 1/108; rebutis, 29/26, oppose, repel
recure, 18/3, redress
reckles, *v.* 32/26, forego (to rakles one's self = to deviate from the proper line of conduct: *Jameson*)
reddyar, 33/84, readier
regaird, *v.* 36/33, look for. Fr. *regarder*
rege, *sb.* 14/50, wantonness, madness
rege, *v.* 28/14, sport lasciviously. Cf. Fr., Cotgrave, *rager*
regiment, 32/9, rule
regioun, 1/187, kingdom
regne, 1/18, reign

106 *Glossary.*

regrat, 36/33 M., regret, complaint
reid, *v.* 33/5, counsel
reidwod, 2/92, furious
reif, *v.* 36/12 ; raifand, 1/125, tear
reik, *v.* 2/134, smoke
reild, *v.* 2/158, rolled
rekless, rekles, 36/2, reckless, careless
releis, 3/48, release, gratification
relȝie, *v.* 32/44, rally
remeid, *sb.* 21/43, 33/5, remedy
remord, *v.* 11/38, have remorse for
remvue, 21/47, remove
rentalis, 1/91, incomes
replaidis, *v.* 36/82 M., ? applies a second time
repleit, *v.* 34/9, replete
reprufe, *v.* 36/59 ; repruif, 36/59 M., reprove
requeir, 35/21, beg
resing, *v.* 30/13, resign
ressauaris, 1/146, takers
ressone, 1/11 ; ressonis, 36/149, reason, arguments
retent, 19/39, retained
reuse, *v.* 32/21 ; rusit, 31/30, praise
revartis, *v.* 3/5 ; rewairt, 21/31 ; rewart, 11/25, 15/19, revive, return, revert
rever, *sb.* 37/10, river
reverend, page 1, line 1, respected
reveris, *sb.* 3/44, a target at an unknown distance from the bowman
rew, *v.* 7/30, 10/30, 24/33 ; rewit, 34/31, pity
rew, *v.* 31/54, 36/36, rue
rewill, *v.* 32/9 ; rewle, *v.* 1/11, rule
rewll, *sb.* 3/21, rule
rewme, 1/147, realm
rewth, *sb.* 21/33, 38/2, pity
rewthfull, 36/52 ; reuthfull, 36/52 M., pityful
richswa, 32/53 ; rycht swa, 36/109, in the same way
richt, 32/12, straight
richtnot of, 21/22, not of right
rin, *v.* 36/35 M. ; ryn, *v.* 36/35, to run
ringis, *v.* 1/188, 27/36 ; rung, 3/25, reigns
rink, 2/42, encounter ; rynk, 31/1, course, race
robbynis, 3/20, ? rustics
rod, 1/11, sceptre
roif, *sb.* 38/83 ; ruve, *sb.* 27/3, rest

roiss, 1/4 ; ross, 8/22, rose
rok, 2/133, distaff
round, *v.* 33/45, talk, whisper. A.S. *runian*
rowtis, 1/188, crowds
rubent, 1/4, ruby-coloured
rubiatouris, 36/83, a term of reproach, rakes. Cf. It. *rubare*, to rob
rufe, *v.* 31/19, rest
ruging, *v.* 1/125, pulling
ruikis, 1/125, rooks
rummyld, *v.* 2/158, made a noise
rumpill, 2/134, rump
rung, 3/25. *See* ringis
rusit. *See* reuse
rute, *v.* 1/111, take root
ruve, *sb.* 27/3, peace
ryce, 1/4, twig. A.S. *Hris*
rycht, *sb.* 1/11, justice
rycht, 1/148, 12/1, 32/12, very, like, in correspondence
ryvis, *v.* 29/27, tears

S

sa, 1/12, 23/20, so
sabill, 12/4, black
saif, *v.* 1/70, save
saif, 36/114, except
saikles, 34/46, without reason
sair, 9/32 ; seir, 1/70, 7/18, sore
sait, 37/4, seat
sall, *v.* 32/56, shall
sallat, 13/8, salad, song, verse
sallis, 25/27, chambers. Fr. *salle*
sanctitude, 1/93, sanctity
sassie, *v.* 36/77. *See* sussy
saule, 29/12 ; saulis, 1/70 ; sawle, 38/9, soul
saw, *v.* 1/174, sow
sawis, 1/193, sayings
schalmis, 2/41, a kind of musical pipe
schankis, 33/30, legs
schaw, *v.* 10/10, 34/22, shew
sched, 4/9, separated. A.S. *sceádan*
scheip, 1/94, sheep
scheir, *v.* 1/174, reap
schene, 11/15, beautiful
schentis, *v.* 29/11 ; schent, 33/18, 36/49, ruins
scherp, 2/17, sharp
scheruitude, 8/18, servitude
scheruiture, 6/17, servitor, servant
scherwand, 11/31, servant

Glossary. 107

schew, *v.* 21/17, shew
scho, 1/213, 2/185, 24/27, 33/17 ; schow, 24/29, she
schoute, *v.* 36/49 M., shout
schute, *v.* 37/11, shoot
scriptouris, 1/171, scriptures
se, 10/21, sea
sedull, 5/33, 34/74 ; scedull, 7/4, writing
seillis, 25/27, ? faggots
seindele, 36/65 M. ; seyndill, 36/65, seldom. Cf. A.S. *syndrian*
seir, 1/70, 7/18, many. *See* sair
seiss, *v.* 1/110, seize, hold
sellis, 31/20, selves
sempill, 1/223, humble
sen, 1/169, since
sent, *v.* 3/40, ? perceive, perhaps scent
senʒeour, 1/157, lord. Fr. *seigneur*
serf, *v.* 8/20, serve
sermondis, 38/19, discourses
sett, 35/17 ; settis, *v.* 33/41, besets
seur, 32/32, sure
sheir, *v.* 1/174, reap
sherp, 2/17, sharp
sic, 22/11, 16, 33/46, such
siching, 13/14, 18/44, sighing
sichis, *v.* 16/19, sighs
sicht, 12/5, 32/10, 18, look, eyesight
sidder, 2/56, ? to place in position
sillie, 1/94 ; silly, 5/26, innocent, simple
sindrye, 1/95 ; sindry, 2/179, sundry
singand, *v.* 1/122, singing
sittelness, 35/17, subtleness
sittin, *v.* 2/35, seated (on his horse)
skaith, 2/53, 9/11, mischief
skant, 34/34, scarcely
skar, 1/211, afraid
skeich, 24/27, skittish
skerss, 19/6, scarce
skraip, *v.* 1/65, gathered
skrufe, 1/65, savings, wealth. A.S. *sceorfan*
sla, *v.* 11/34, slay
slaid, *v.* 2/65, slid
slaik, *v.* 18/44, cease
slak, 2/167, opening, hill road
sle, 25/3, sly
slicht, *adj.* 32/title, simple
slicht, *sb.* 33/69, knowledge, craft
smaragde, 1/220, emerald. L. *smaragdus*
smartit, *v.* 36/50, pained

smeir, *v.* 1/94, smear, or ? to choke. Cf. A.S. *smorian*
smit, 1/220, particle, trace. A.S. *smitan*
smot, *sb.* 1/220, mouldiness, stain
smot, *v.* 31/52 ; smote, 36/16 M. ; smyte, *v.* 36/16, smut, stain
snaw, 38/31, snow
sneir, *v.* 1/190, sail rapidly.
sobir, 5/7, unpretending
sodomeitis, 36/115, sodomites
soir, 1/12, 33/20, badly, sorely
soletare, 32/16, alone
solist, *v.* 1/158, 32/41, solicit
sollesing, 16/43, solacing
sonnest, 33/85, soonest
sorcereis, 1/93, *sb. pl.* of sorcery, magic
sould, *v.* 1/194 ; suld, 2/78, should
soun, 13/14, fainting
sounʒe, *v.* 36/93 ; sunʒe, 36/93 M., take an interest in. Cf. Fr. *soigner*
sovirlie, 38/52, certainly, surely
spanʒeollis, 33/26, spaniels
speiche, 32/47, speech
speir, *v.* 33/31, ask. Icel. *spyrja*
spill, *v.* 2/182, 15/24, spoil, mar
spreit, 37/30, 38/51, spirit
spreitles, 13/33, spiritless
spune, *v.* 31/7, spun
stabill, *v.* 1/41, establish ; *adj.* 7/26, stable
staffage, 19/17, stiffish, obstinate
staige, 13/2, in staige, step by step
staik, *v.* 30/32, satisfy
stait, 1/170, profession
stalf, 2/66, staff
stall, *v.* 2/52, stole
stanche, *v.* 1/41, staunch
start, *v.* 11/24 ; stairtis, 7/7, shrink away, starts
stayne, 36/45 M., stone
steir, *v.* 1/30, 27/43, steer
steir, *sb.* 2/101, on steir = astir
steir, *sb.* 13/25, guide
stervis, *v.* 7/32, dies
stoir, 37/31, store
stoundis, *v.* 12/6, strikes. Cf. A.S. *stund*
stowin, *v.* 2/66, stolen
strange, 19/18, distant
stro, 37/19, straw
strynd, 32/5, strain, race
sturt, 29/14, vexation
styme, 29/23, faint form, object

styngis, 2/52, spears. A.S. *sting*
sua, 33/69; swa, 32/46, 36/93, so
suaif, 8/29, sweet
sueir, *v.* 35/14, swear
sueit, 17/35, sweet
sulfurius, 27/39, sulphurous
sum, 2/156, 33/73, one; 11/8, some
supplant, *v.* 36/48, to get the better of
suppois, *conj.* 3/35, 7/2, 22/17, 33/103, although
suppone, *v.* 1/203, suppose, assume
suspectit, *v.* 34/46, *pp.* suspect
sussy, *v.* 31/22, 36/77; sassie, 36/77 M., care; sussy, *sb.* 13/9, care
suth, *adj.* 1/193, true; 25/20, *sb.* truth
swaif, *adv.* 1/214, sweetly
swerd, 1/172, sword
swyvis, 33/36, *sb. pl.* copulation
syiss, 11/2, 37/23, times. O.E. *sithes*
sympilness, *sb.* 5/23, humble rank
syn, 2/73, sun
synd, *v.* 17/38, ? sundered, quenched, perhaps—washed away
syndrie, 36/43 M., sundry
syne, 37/23, sin
syne, 1/84, 34/22, 36/78, then
synis, 32/17, signs
syte, *sb.* 36/38; sytt, *sb.* 13/9, grief, mourning. Icel. *syta*

T

taist, *v.* 10/25, try. O.Fr. *taster*
taikles, 12/20, without tackle
tane, *v.* 31/2, 35/9, taken
targe, 1/207, shield
techit, *v. pp.* 1/115, taught
ted, *v.* 19/23, turned (to tede grass = to turn or spread abroad new mown grass : *N. Bailey's Dict.*)
teindis, 1/133, tithes
temerat, 31/37, timorous
temper, *v.* 1/31, moderate
tene, 38/14, trouble. A.S. *téon*
tennentis, *sb. pl.* 1/139, tenants
tent, 1/59, 33/23, care
test, *v.* 27/14, taste
tha, 2/15, those
thad, 2/166, that
thair, 35/22, 36/125; thir, 1/137, 2/21, 30/49, these
thairout, 36/25, anywhere
thaj, 1/59; the, 37/22, they
thay, 36/32; tha, 2/15; þe, 29/25, those

thing, *v.* 30/15, to fornicate with
thir, 1/137, these
thirlaige, 13/4, thraldom
thirlit, *adj.* 12/1, 16/26, pierced
this, 17/2, thus
thocht, 31/37, though
thoill, *v.* 6/18, 11/16, 24/15; thoillis, 15/18, suffer
thra, 11/31, obstinate
thrissill, 1/3, thistle
throw, 2/50, through
till, 1/28, 2/141, 33/21, 32/47, to
tod, 25/29, fox
toft, 19/23, tuft
togiddir, 36/24, together
topas, 12/11, topaz
traik, 1/59, ? idle wandering, perhaps business
trane, 28/21, 36/44, 75, 35/10, train, enticement
trateis, *sb.* 36/44 M.; 36/44, trattillis, tales, stories
trattill, *v.* 36/73, prattle
traittilis, *sb.* 36/44, prattle
tray, 38/14, trouble, vexation
treit, *v.* 1/166, treat
tremebund, 34/56, timorous. L. *tremebundus*
trenefald, 38/82, threefold
trentalis, 1/89, a service for the dead which consisted of thirty masses
trest, 15/6, 30/8, faithful
trest, *v.* 36/39; traist, 36/39 M., trust
trewth, 34/33, truth
trincher, 2/46, cutting
trollie-lolly, 33/61, membrum virile
trowit, *v.* 34/33, believed
tryme, 14/53, trim
tummyll, *v.* 36/80, tumble
tuk, *v.* 2/188, took
tvme, 1/89, empty
turcas, 12/11, turquoise
twche, 2/139, tough
tyd, 19/38, time. A.S. *tid*
tymis, 3/22, times
tymmer wechtis, *sb. pl.* 3/9, tabor, tamborine
tyne, *v.* 27/5, 35/23; tynt, *v.* 2/44, lose. Icel. *týna*
tyrit, 1/89, tired
tyst, *v.* 36/73; tyist, 36/73 M., entice

V

vagis, *v.* 36/89 M. See *waggis*
vane, 7/34, vein

Glossary. 109

vaneist, *v.* 37/20, vanished, blown away
verry, 7/39, 27/45, true
vertewus, 1/25, virtues
veschell, 31/4, vessel
vesy, *v.* 24/26. *See* wisy
vitious, 1/58, vicious
vg, *v.* 36/119, feel abhorrence at
vncurtass, 19/19, uncourteous
vndantit, *v.* 31/11, unbroken
vndegraid, 12/13, having no degrees or limits
vndir coite, 36/150, under cloak, secret
vnhapp, 36/123, unlucky. Icel. *u-happ*
vnleill, 21/25, 34/7, disloyal
vnrycht, *sb.* 30/9, without due reason
vnsellis, *sb.* 34/19, worthless persons. A.S. *unsealig*
vntil, 37/5, unto
vnwyce, 27/23, unwise
vpcoill, 3/10, a game with balls (*Jamieson*)
vp, 36/64 ; vpe, 36/64 M., up
vpliftis, *v.* 1/147, exacts, collects, grabs
vpross, *v.* 14/26, oppress
vptane, *v.* 1/133, uptaken, collected
vyce, *sb.* 36/103, device

W

wa, 11/30, 23/21, woe
wache, 13/38, watch
waggis, 36/89 ; vagis, 36/89 M., wander or roam with (cf. Fr. *vaguer*, to wander: *Cotgrave*)
waik, *v.* 3/23, watch
waikis, *v.* 36/14, weakens
wair, *v.* 20/5, spend
wa iss ȝow, 36/151, woe is you
waist, 10/25, waste
wait, *v.* 37/25, know
wald, *v.* 1/57, would
walking, 13/15, waking
wallowit, 12/16, faded. A.S. *wealwian*
walteris, 3/37, waters
walx, 1/105, wax
wame, 36/79, 33/27, belly. A.S. *wamb*
wanhap, 34/27, mishap
wanrest, 18/36, 55, unrest
wantage, 25/2, advantage
wappit, *v.* 18/3, wrapped

war, *v.* 3/23, 33/78 ; wes, *v.* 2/3 ; wer, *v.* 5/17, was, were
war, 32/19, 38, 35/1, wary
war, *v.* 36/151, beware
waresone, 5/3, reward
wariand, 24/38, varying, shifting
warld, 1/58, world
wary, *v.* 36/55 ; warye, 36/55 M., curse
wating, 34/61, waiting
watt, *v.* 32/38, pursue, lie in wait for. O.Fr. *waiter*
wattis, *v.* 1/82 ; wait, 9/12, 13, 14/8, 16/17, 37/25 ; wat, 31/39, 34/73 ; wit, 32/19 ; wittin, *pp.* 2/29 ; witting, *pres. p.* 11/14, to know
waye, *v.* 1/29, weigh
wayiss, *sb.* 2/53, way, manner
wechtis, *sb. pl.* 3/9, usually an instrument for winnowing corn: in this place *wecht* means a kind of tambourine
weddir-skynis, 2/116, sheep-skins
wedow men, 33/35, widowers
weddow, 32/55, widow
weid, 31/7, dress
weill, *adv.* 11/20, 14/36, 17/20, *adj.* well
weill, *sb.* 15/32, weal
weir, 1/126 ; weiris, 2/13, war. A.S. *werian*
weir, *v.* 2/105, to defend
weit, *v.* 3/70, wet, moisten
wem, 24/3, stain
went, *v.* 13/38, 24/19, wend, go
werd, 21/11, fate
werrie, 1/126, ? vexatious, or ? very
werst, 29/41, worst
wes (*see* war)
wesche, *v.* 38/9, wash
wicht, 13/24, 14/8, wight
wichttar, 2/30, weightier, stronger
wid, *adj.* 31/17, mad
wie, 9/31 ; wy, 27/27, 32/39, wight, applied to man or woman
wilrone, 36/106 ; wilroun, 36/106 M., wild boar
wilsum, 16/22, wandering
winche, 25/1, wench
wirk, *v.* 30/20, 32/55, work
wirschep, 1/28 ; 31/23, honour
wiss, 34/34, wish
wisy, *v.* 1/151 ; vesy, 24/26, examine, supervise. L. *visere*
wit, *sb.* 36/23, intelligence

Glossary.

witt, *v.* 1/159; wyt, 15/8, 34/73; wyte, 1/57, chide
wittin, *v.* 2/29, known
woles, 32/28, woeless, painless
wolffe, 36/106 M., wolf
woltir, *v.* 36/80 M., turn; woltir oure, turn over. A.S. *wealtan*
womanheid, 9/16, 33/4, womanhood
womenting, 32/8, lamentation
wont, 20/38, weened, supposed
wow, *v.* 5/38, avow
wowaris, 36/89, wooers
wowbattis, *sb. pl.* 36/94, a decayed rake
woyd, 13/17, void
wrangus, 1/151, unjust, wrongful
wrangusly, 18/34, wrongly
wreth, 32/30, wrath
wrocht, *v.* 1/151, 5/30, worked; 32/39, created
ws, 1/15, 13/40, us

wvne, *v.* 31/3, won
wy. *See* wie
wyiss, *adj.* 32/38; wysest, 36/25; wyisast, 36/25 M., wise
wyiss, 33/74, manner
wyle, *v.* 30/27; wyllit, *v.* 36/26; wylit, *v.* 36/26 M., allure
wyle, *sb.* 35/15; wylis, 32/38, allurements
wylie, 25/29, sly
wyn, *v.* 32/48, obtain
wyte, *sb.* 36/129, blame. A.S. *witan*
wyvis, 33/37, women

ȝ

ȝeid, *v.* 3/16, went
ȝeir, 1/11, year
ȝit, 1/62, 36/34 M., yet
ȝoung, 36/81 M.; ȝung, 36/81, young
ȝunkeirs, 2/37, young men

PROPER NAMES.

I. PERSONS.

Adame, 5/16
Adamsone, Wm., 2/30

Bruce, Robert, 1/196; b. about 1274, became joint regent of Scotland in 1299. After the murder of Comyn on March 27th, 1306, he was crowned King of Scotland at Scone. He suffered defeat at the hands of Edward I. of England, and had to take refuge in the Western Isles. After a long struggle he recaptured most of the Scottish strongholds, and in 1314, at Bannockburn, he totally defeated the forces of Edward II. Fourteen years later peace was made between Scotland and England. Robert Bruce died June 7th, 1329

Christ, 1/201, 17/17
Cupid, 13/11, 19/29, 22/8, 9, 29/2; Cupeid, 36/41; Cupide, 36/41 M.

Dyane, 12/3

Erskyn, Maister of, 16/title (see note)
Eue, 5/16; Eua, 36/128

Frances, 1/198, born at Fontainebleau in 1544, was married to Mary Stuart, daughter of James V. of Scotland, in 1558. He became King of France in 1559, and died in December 1560

Gemyny, 3/30, the twins, the third sign of the Zodiac, named after the two brightest stars, Castor and Pollux. The sun is in Gemini from about May 21st till about June 21st

Grissal, 17/7, the heroine of a popular medieval tale; a Piedmontese peasant girl, who was married by the Marquis of Saluzzo. To test her character, her husband made her submit to many cruel tests. Her children were taken from her to be killed, so she was told; finally she was ordered to return to her peasant home. All the harsh treatment she bore without a murmur. At length her husband, convinced of her devotion, restored her to her position, and gave her back her children, and lived happily with her for many years

Hercules, 2/7
Hoid, Robene, 3/17

Johne, Littill, 3/17, the companion of Robin Hood
Jok, 2/129, the brother of Will

Littill Johne, 3/17, a comrade of Robin Hood

Mars, 2/5
Mary, 1/title; born on Dec. 7th or 8th, 1542, at Linlithgow Palace, a few days before the death of her father, James V. She was proclaimed queen, and on Sept. 9th, 1543, was crowned at Stirling Castle by Cardinal Beaton. She

left Scotland on Aug. 7th, 1548, for the court of France: she was married to the Dauphin on April 24th, 1558, and became Queen of France the following year. On Aug. 25th, 1560, the Roman hierarchy was disestablished in Scotland. Her husband, Francis II., died Dec. 5, 1560. After unsuccessful attempts by her relatives to negociate a marriage with Charles IX., King of France, the brother of her late husband, and afterwards with Don Carlos of Spain, she returned to Scotland on Aug. 15th, 1561. She was pledged not to interfere with the religious system which there obtained, though she retained freedom to exercise her own form of worship. This pledge she did not keep. Mary occupied much of her energy in prosecuting her claim to the English throne. She was married to Lord Darnley in the Chapel at Holyrood on June 29th, 1565. Two years after he was assassinated, and she married James Hepburn, fourth Earl of Bothwell, on May 15th, 1567, who was publicly asserted to be guilty of the crime. On the 24th of July following, she was compelled to abdicate, and was kept a prisoner at Lochleven Castle. She escaped on March 2, 1568, and attempted to regain her position. Her supporters were defeated at Langside on May 13, and three days after she crossed the Solway to England, where she remained until her execution on Feb. 8th, 1586-7

Mawis, 23/22, Magdalen
Meg, 23/22, Margaret
Meriory, 23/22, Marjory

Pasifie, 36/114, the wife of Minos, and mother of the Minatour
Paull, 1/153
Phebus, 3/30, 12/2, Phœbus the bright, an epithet and name given to Apollo, who became identified with Helios the sun-god

Robene Hoid, 3/17, the hero of Sherwood and Barnsdale Forests. A bold outlaw, who took from the rich and gave to the poor. Sir Walter Scott represents him as a Saxon chief, who held out against the Normans
Sanct Blais, 1/86, the patron of Pladay, a small island off the coast of Arran (cf. *Fordun*, I. 6, II. 10)
Sanct Boit, 1/86, probably Bathan (also known as Bathanus, Baithonus, Bothanus), a Scotch saint. His name is mentioned in the Epistle to the Scots by Pope Julius IV., 639 A.D. The parish of Gifford or Yester, in East Lothian, was at one time called St. Bothans. The parish of Bowden is said to take its name from this saint (cf. A. P. Forbes, *Kalendars of Scottish Saints*, 1872). There is also a saint named Baitin. He was cousin-german of Saint Columba; he accompanied his cousin to Scotland, and for a time presided over the monastery of Magh Lunge in Tiree. He was devoted to agriculture and transcribing books. On St. Columba's death Baitan was his successor, and held office about four years. He died circa 600 (cf. Adamnan's *Vita S. Columbae*, ed. Reeves, 1857).
"Thanks to Saint Bothan, son of mine,
Save Gawain, ne'er could pen a line."—Scott's *Marmion*, vi. 15.
Sanct Dauidis, 1/122
Satane, 27/46
Scott, Sanderris, 1/223, 26/title, 31/56, 36/152
Syme, Johnie, 2/31

Venus, 3/2, 14/52, 22/6, 30/7, 31/7, 36/42, 88

William Adamsone, title/2; Will, 2/15, a combatant at the jousting at The Drum

II. PLACES.

Albion, 1/6, a name of Great Britain

Bretane, 1/194, 206, Great Britain

Dalkeith, 2/91, 99
Drum, 2/9, now Somerville House, near Dalkeith

Europ, 1/188

Inche-bukling-bray, 3/59, a hill a short distance from Musselburgh, between that town and Haddington
Italie, 36/117

Jerusalem, 38/75

Lareit, 3/56, the chapel of Our Lady of Lorretto was situated at the east end of the town of Musselburgh. It was destroyed by the Earl of Hertford in May 1544, though afterward it was repaired. In 1590 it was finally abolished. Of this celebrated chapel only a small burial vault now remains

Lorane, 1/3, Lorraine
Lumbardie, 36/116, Lombardy

Mussilburch, 3/60, Musselburgh, a town near Edinburgh, on the Esk

Naippillis, 36/116, Naples

Potter-raw, 2/178, an old street on the south side of Edinburgh, which at the time of Alexander Scott was outside the city wall. At the north end of the street was Potter-raw Port

Rome, 36/116

The manufacturer's authorised representative in the EU for product safety is Oxford University Press España S.A. of el Parque Empresarial San Fernando de Henares, Avenida de Castilla, 2 – 28830 Madrid (www.oup.es/en or product.safety@oup.com). OUP España S.A. also acts as importer into Spain of products made by the manufacturer.

www.ingramcontent.com/pod-product-compliance
Ingram Content Group UK Ltd.
Pitfield, Milton Keynes, MK11 3LW, UK
UKHW041902230426
12049UKWH00001B/4